Endless Love

Overcoming Adversity to Relentlessly Love God, Intentionally Love Yourself, and Authentically Love Others

Written by Angela Moore

WWW.COUNTLESSLOVE.COM

DISCLAIMER

Although the author and publisher have made every effort to ensure that the information in this book was correct at press time, the author does not assume and hereby disclaims any liability to any party for any loss, damage, or disruption caused by errors, or omissions, whether such errors or omissions result from negligence, accident, or any other cause.

Author further disclaims any liability for any party for the self-help advice and opinions on said subjects contained within this book. The information provided in this book is designed to provide helpful information on the subjects discussed. This book is not meant to be used, nor should it be used, to diagnose or treat any medical condition.

DEDICATION

dedicate this book to all those rooted in bitterness and rejection, but still standing. To those who've broken from the thorns of life but are still recovering. To those who are living with stains from unbelief, doubt, oppression, depression, racism, discrimination, abuse, and trauma, but still going strong. You are the author of your story. Don't allow others to dictate the script. You identify the starring characters. Each day is a new opportunity to reset, restart, renew.

TABLE OF CONTENTS

CHAPTER THREE

CHAPTER FOUR

CONCLUSION

INTRODUCTION
DISCOVERING ENDLESS LOVE

"Love is the emblem of eternity; it confounds all notion of time; effaces all memory of a beginning, all fear of an end."
— **Madame de Stael**

hid my feelings for years. I knew I was living a lie, but I didn't know what to do or who to turn to. I smiled and held my peace and practiced the same plastic smile and familiar routine. I got up, went to work, took care of dinner and the kids, went to sleep, and did it all again the next day. Every day was as familiar as the last, except I was slowly drifting even deeper into a pit of despair. I wasn't okay, and I knew it.

When it was just me and the kids, the mood was usually calm besides the minor issues kids have. Whenever I encountered certain friends and family members, I felt the weight of the world on my shoulders. They took my love, sincerity, and honor for granted. I freely loved them, freely honored them, and wanted the best for them. Their love came with conditions, while I did my best to love unconditionally. I was nowhere near perfect, but I showed love.

I couldn't meet or maintain the conditions of attention and affection that required me to neglect my needs. I submerged my time and energy into pleasing everyone else around me as I continued to suffer. My needs were lacking, and no one was coming to my rescue. No one was knocking at my door to check on me. I was dying on the inside with no end in sight. Each day felt like a revolving door with my life slipping away before my eyes, and there was nothing I could do to slow it down.

Why didn't I have the courage to say how I felt? Why did I let the cruel behavior go on for so long? Why didn't I stand up for myself? These are great questions I felt in my heart but had no answers for at the time. These types of questions rarely find answers right away because your mind is putting up a defense to convince you everything is okay, even when it's not.

Of course, life wasn't all bad. The occasional smiles and spurts of friendly encounters helped bring me back to the surface. Bitter hellos and silent goodbyes were the norm, but there were specks of brightness in the dark. These small sparks renewed my hope that something better was around the corner. The wait was just longer than I expected and almost more than I could handle.

I wanted someone to rescue me, but no one came. I went to church seeking refuge, and I prayed endlessly day and night. I remember many days of depression and feelings of exhaustion from seeking a way out of my situation. I didn't understand why God didn't rescue me and take care of his child. Why wouldn't he just scoop me up and set me free? It would be so easy for Him. These moments where I had to stay put and fight challenged my faith and strengthened me. If you stay strong and keep looking up, God always comes through. He will always set us free in Him.

During one particularly challenging season, I distinctly remember kneeling in my room praying the following prayer:

I am here God! Mrs. Faithful, your humble servant: lover, giver and submissive servant. Where are you, God? Why aren't you showing up in my life? What am I supposed to do now? Why am I dealing with all this pain and craziness? Help me, please! Don't leave me here all alone.

Growing up, I wasn't taught how-to walk-in freedom. Fear and intimidation were the clothes I wore every day. Family traditions and religion passed down this way of life. It taught me to follow the given path without a harsh reality, but it was all I knew.

I discovered throughout my journey that traditions and religion kept me in a box and kept me bound to an unfulfilled life. These very traditions caused me to unquestionably follow him when I should have run away and gotten help. The women in the generation before me kept their mouths closed, did as they were told, and worked endlessly to please their men and their family. They used their religion to mask their pain and give hope to their lack of love and support. This was not a path I wanted to follow, but I was already on it and momentum is hard to stop.

I feared challenging the traditions that were passed down to me by my grandparents because I thought it was a sin. Imagine that! I thought it was a sin to speak my mind and share my opinion. Wow! For years, my life stayed in a loop, changing every day but not really changing at all. All I could do was adapt to new situations and circumstances as they came. I feared addressing the root cause of any problem because of the fear I lived with. I dealt with it simply by ignoring the problem and hoping it would work itself out. Of course, that's not how things work. Life is never that easy.

> *It's very, very simple to get what you want, but it's not easy. It's your job to make yourself do the crap you don't want to do, so you can be everything that you're supposed to be. And you're so damn busy waiting 'to feel like it.' And you're never going to – ever. No one's coming. No one. No one's coming to push you; no one's coming to tell you to turn the TV off; no one's coming to tell you to get out the door and exercise; nobody's coming to tell you to apply for that job that you've always dreamt about; nobody's coming to write the business plan for you. It's up to you.*

> **— Mel Robbins, Bestselling author and speaker[1]**

No one cared that I was uncomfortable, and no one cared that I was unfulfilled. I internalized so much pain; I became

---

[1] Robbins, Mel. "How to Stop Screwing Yourself Over." TED Talks, uploaded by TEDxTalks, 28 Mar. 2018, www.ted.com/talks/mel_robbins_how_to_stop_screwing_yourself_over?language=en.

https://www.ted.com/talks/mel_robbins_how_to_stop_screwing_yourself_over?language=en

physically sick and mentally exhausted. I knew it was time for me to make a change, fearful or not, ready or not. It was now or never. I finally realized the help I was looking for was in me all along. I no longer needed anyone to tell me to pursue a better life. I shifted my mindset and told myself daily:

"You will live and not die."

This simple phrase kept me going. Knowing I would live and get through my current hell gave me hope. Of course, this change didn't happen overnight, and I still struggled to get by. But the daily practice of repeating this affirmation helped me to push myself through to victory. I told myself this short phrase every single morning as I stood in front of the bathroom mirror. It required intense focus to be free from the oppression of my past, but little by little, I was getting better.

Today, I am free from fear, intimidation, lack of resources, lack of understanding, and lack of faith. With God's help, I have finally overcome fear. I am a new creature; I am the woman God has created me to be. I am not who or what a man or anyone else says that I am. I am not limited by the standards of this world, and I know God created me for such a time as this. I will not stop, and I will not be ashamed of my past.

I want the same for you. It starts with love. Use this story to take authority over the direction of your life. Let today be your day of greatness to manifest beyond what you could ever think, ask, or even imagine.

LEARNING TO LOVE

I met my children's father when I was fifteen and then I got pregnant at sixteen. To say it devastated me would be a monumental understatement. I was seeing my future pass by before my eyes, and I hated what I saw. But this only made me want to fight even harder. My journey and my change started with building a relationship with God and learning how to love. I started reading the Bible more frequently and praying more often. The adults in my life weren't providing guidance or direction, so I read the Bible even though I didn't understand every word. I didn't have anyone in my life as a mentor, so I followed the only voice I could.

In my early twenties, I started journaling, and this led me to keep seeking healing and change. My kids and I got even more involved in church and joined several ministries. This really helped me meet different people who had the knowledge and wisdom to help me. I ran into some good and bad people in church. But overall, my relationship with God grew, and it strengthened me mentally, emotionally, and spiritually. I was fortunate to be in the company of some good people who, for once in my life, actually had my best interests at heart.

There are so many books you can read that will show you how to improve your life. Some books will even say you can do it in thirty days or less by forming new habits. Yeah, right! It takes years to lose yourself, realize your life is a hot mess, and seek a solution to initiate healing. Awareness is the first step toward learning to love, but it comes at a cost. Suddenly, you realize just how blind you were, and the need to escape to greener pastures is even more imperative. This is true of any life change, but particularly difficult when you are living in difficult circumstances. This sudden clarity doesn't grant immediate results, but it shows you how far you need to go. This is when you need to sink your toes into the sand and stand firm.

I exhausted myself reading several books and talking to multiple therapists about my problems. Yes, it was a necessary part of my journey, but I wish it didn't have to go on so long! It was so depressing regurgitating the same painful events of my life over and over again. Eventually, I realized I needed to find a solution, but I still had so many questions, such as:

- How do I love God like I know I'm supposed to?

- How do I find balance in love and find time for God, myself, and for others?

- How do I show love to other people even when they don't deserve it?

- When everything around me looks and sounds like hell, how do I still reach for heaven?

The answer to these questions? Love. It's simple yet challenging. It's easy, yet incredibly difficult. It's the very thing you need to improve, but the last thing you think you need.

Learning to love was an arduous process because I thought that life was supposed to go a certain way according to what other people told me. I thought that what I saw on TV was real life. I was told to follow a process, and I assumed it would generate what I wanted. I didn't think to ask the above questions because nobody else in my life was asking them either. I saw the world in black and white, but I've since learned we are all unique in many important ways.

We may have similarities, but we all serve a different purpose. Someone that performs poorly in school could be a dynamic entrepreneur later on in life. Someone who aces every test might be perfect for a government research job. We all know several stories of someone dropping out of college and pursuing their passion and becoming wildly successful. What works for me may not work for you and vice versa. Understanding who you are and what moves you is part of learning to love because you then pass this understanding over to your relationships with others.

Practicing Endless Love is about loving God with all your heart, mind and soul, loving yourself, and loving your neighbor who is different from you as you learn to love yourself. Then, as you embrace love in your heart, you make treasure out of whatever trash you're dealt. It's not easy, but it's necessary as you seek to be a person of continuous, energetic, and Endless Love.

This short book and the following lessons are only for minds and hearts ready for change. I don't have all the answers to life, but this is my story. To learn to love with all of your heart takes a willingness to open up your heart and feel! This opening of your heart can be painful, and you might feel you'd rather avoid the discomfort. I've found that some of life's best moments are part of the upswing after an especially grueling experience. But you must be open to the experience, whether it takes you up to the stars or deep down into anguish. My journey shows how life handed me trash, but I discovered treasure. It shows how I learned to love despite a myriad of things I had to overcome. I'll share how Endless Love brought a heightened sense of fulfillment to my life, gave me hope for a better future, and might do the same for you.

THERE IS ALWAYS HOPE

At one point, I was so fragile, I couldn't handle confrontations and I couldn't express myself without crying or having an outburst. I was overly sensitive. I would let things bother me to where I wouldn't be able to sleep for days. I was an emotional basket case. I started seeing a therapist and found people I could talk to about what was going on with me. I started reading books about deliverance, hope, and self-improvement. I became extremely close with a husband-and-wife pastor team who invited me to their home for prayer every Saturday and Sunday (I was there every time their door was open). I made going to church a huge part of my life because I knew I needed to be around like-minded people. I filled my life with prayer, church, and meditation. I went hard for about three years straight and learned a ton about myself in this timeframe.

I learned that I'm not that same scared, timid, shy, emotionally wounded little girl anymore. It took some time for me to get here and I'm still pursuing a better version of myself every day. As long as I have my health and strength, I'm going to continue to be better and do better.

If you're struggling to get started and are feeling hopeless, one of the very best things you can do is start reading. So, good on you for picking up this book! I hope it becomes a catalyst for new life, direction, and renewed hope. Reading is a surefire way to trigger fresh thoughts and prompt positive action. It increases resilience and makes you more able to respond to difficult situations and circumstances. People who read find the circuits and signals in their brain strengthening over time,[2] and it's worked wonders for me.

I'll break the norm and share other self-improvement books that have helped me right here in the introduction. Add these books to your reading list right after you finish this one:

1. *The Power of Positive Thinking* by Norman Vincent Peale

2. *Shift into a Higher Gear* by Delaro McNeal II

---

[2] Houston, Suzanne M et al. "Reading skill and structural brain development." Neuroreport vol. 25,5 (2014): 347-52. doi:10.1097/WNR.0000000000000121

3. *As a Man Thinketh* by James Allen

4. *The Secret* by Rhonda Byrne

5. *The Four Agreements* by Don Miguel Ruiz

6. *Battlefield of the Mind* by Joyce Myers

As you grow your mind and put into practice the methods I will share in this book, you will learn that your mentality and the way you think are extremely important. In fact, it's the way God designed us! He gave us an organic mega-computer right inside our heads so that we could understand and communicate with him. But it's up to us to turn on the dials to read and receive what God is telling us if we even hope to find peace in our hearts.

FINDING INNER PEACE

Most people look at love as a noun or adjective; it's described as a beauty, a feeling or an emotion. Love is much greater and deeper than your emotions and your feelings. It's a necessity for every human being. Without love, you cannot live. It shapes and models your character, your emotions, your mental stability, and your outlook on life. Many people fear love, but genuine love opens you up to vulnerability. Love requires a duality of self-awareness and selflessness. This process might sound intimidating, but we will practice it together.

When we love absolutely, we come face to face with inner peace and it's a glorious feeling. Practice love in order to improve and to find this inner peace. I'll share my best strategies for living out love in a real and practical way. You'll learn from my struggles and failures, and I'll share what is working for me right now to grow closer to God, understand myself, and show Endless Love to all people despite hardship and tough circumstances.

IN THE FOUR CHAPTERS OF THIS BOOK, YOU WILL DISCOVER:

1. The joy of putting God first and strategies for the daily practice of keeping Him front and center.

2. Why it is vital to practice self-love and how it will make you a better and ultimately less selfish person.

3. How to love others to the best of your ability by understanding and falling in love with our differences.

4. The right way to deal with adversity and overcome obstacles.

Love is an action word. Love is all around us. Love is pain and joy. Love is sadness and peace. Love is insecurity and hope. Love is Endless yet it can be so hard to find. Love is your ticket to true and lasting inner peace. Unlock Endless Love in your life and this peace will come upon you like the rays from the sun on a brand-new morning.

Once I decided I no longer wanted to hide who I was, healing came to me. It seems easy to suffer in silence, but it's actually much harder! We all desire the same basic needs to sustain life: safety, security, and stability. We all desire peace, both internally and externally. But it doesn't start pain free. To start a journey of healing, you must realize you're sick. Self-awareness is the absolute first step you must take. There is no other way.

You must look at yourself and be honest about where you are. Inner peace will never find you if you don't admit you need it. Where are you mentally, emotionally, and physically? Are you loving God, yourself, and others to the best of your ability? If not, you must start in the area where you are lacking. If you struggle with putting God first, start there. If you need to show yourself the love you deserve, take the time to do so. If you know you need to show love to others, practice today. If you know you struggle to take action on the things you learn, start small and do something simple but potentially life-changing right now. I'll help you along the way but start with what you already know you need to do.

Affirmations and prayers helped me greatly in my journey, and you will find many in the back of this book. Use these as a resource and you come back to often. Please write in this book and jot down notes. Use the material to grow and change and become love. Take the time you need and make progress each day toward inner peace.

My healing process took time, and it will take time for you, too. It wasn't easy, but I never gave up. I worked to better understand and control my emotions and mental health. I endured mental and emotional trauma for years. Today, I can finally say I am emotionally and mentally stable. I am ready to share my story. I hope you cherish it, feel the love, and ultimately discover how to fill your life with Endless Love.

In Romans 12:2 (one of the books in the Bible) it says:

> *Do not be conformed to this world, but be transformed by the renewal of your mind, that by testing you may discern what is the will of God, what is good and acceptable and perfect. [Rom 12:2 ESV]*

You are in God's good, pleasing, and perfect will, and you are well on your way to living out Endless Love. I am so glad you found your way here. Let's get started.

PRACTICING ENDLESS LOVE

In each chapter in this book, I will present you with three action steps to complete after reading. If reading from a print book, check these boxes with a pen. If reading on an eBook, don't dent your screen. Instead, mentally check off each item after you complete them.

- **Pray:** *Lord, give me the strength and wisdom I need to tackle each day. Give me the time and opportunity to finish reading this book and to do what you would have me do. Be with me as I learn how to love you more deeply, love* *myself more kindly, and love others with increased vigor. Thank you for being my Lord and protector. Amen!*

- **Read:** Pick one book mentioned in this introduction and add it to your reading list today.

- **Act:** Grow in self-awareness today and think about the ways you need Endless Love to enter your heart. Take a deep breath and spend five minutes filling your mind with positive thoughts. Consider your best next loving action towards God, yourself, or another person. Act on what you discover and use it to take action in love today.

CHAPTER ONE
SEEKING SERENITY: RELENTLESSLY LOVING GOD ABOVE ALL ELSE

> *'And you shall love the Lord your God with all your heart and with all your soul and with all your mind and with all your strength.' The second is this: 'You shall love your neighbor as yourself.' There is no other commandment greater than these. [Mark 12:30-31 ESV]*

was thirteen when my mother lost her husband to the streets. I remember walking into the house on that fateful day with my six-year-old-sister. As she walked into his room and saw him lying on the bed with his eyes and mouth open, she yelled, "What's wrong with my daddy!?," at the top of her lungs. I immediately jumped up from the couch and followed her distressed voice into the room. Her words struck fear into my heart, mixed with what I now know was a bit of hope, as ashamed as I am to admit it even now.

I stood over his lifeless body, waiting for him to move, but there were no signs of movement. His lips were blue, and his skin pale. I stood there waiting to see if his body would take in air, but I didn't notice any breathing. At that moment, I knew he was gone. I felt relief from years of heaviness. The burden of abuse was suddenly taken from me. I felt like God had finally vindicated me. I felt no remorse or sympathy for this man as his body laid there lifeless.

I spun away, grabbed my sister's hand, and told her we were going for a walk. We walked all the way to my aunt's house and called my mother. She picked up the phone, and I remember saying coolly, "Something's wrong with your husband. You need to get home." She asked questions, but all I could recall was the needle on the floor and how lifeless his body appeared. I knew he was gone, but I didn't have the words or the wherewithal to tell her.

On the way home that same evening, I remember coming around the corner to the street we lived on and there was a crowd of people standing in front of our building. It felt like every neighbor on the block was in front of our building. The door to our building was wide open. Two men carrying a stretcher carefully pushed his lifeless body to the ambulance truck as we waded through the crowd of nosy neighbors. As we approached the building, everyone turned to look at us and softly asked as we walked by, "Are you okay?" "Okay?" I thought. "I don't know what to feel…"

When you seek a place of quiet reflection, God will be there waiting for you. The creator will speak to you and reveal his true self whenever and wherever you find that peaceful place of serenity. He is always ready and eager to hear from His children! He has a way to meet you and show you love wherever you might be, intellectually, emotionally, and spiritually.

It doesn't matter if you've never read the Bible or have been going to church since you were a toddler, the Lord can and will reach you if you are open and willing to hear from Him, even if (and especially if!) you are struggling.

When I was growing up, my mom worked a lot and put a lot of responsibility on me. I looked out for my younger sister, while my mom worked two jobs. She didn't have the time to nurture us or provide guidance. I struggled with bullying, low self-esteem, and depression. My dad stopped talking to me at fifteen. My mom married her husband when I was around eleven. He wasn't caring or affectionate towards me and he would occasionally say a lot of hurtful things to me, particularly when I would make mistakes. Children are like sponges, they are constantly soaking up their environments, whether the environments are good or bad. They will repeat what they see and what they hear, and they don't come with instructions or manuals.

Throughout my life, I've faced many struggles and unfair situations. No child should have to look upon the face of death, nonetheless, be thankful in that moment! The insanity of what I dealt with still hits me hard, even to this day. It wasn't fair, nor was it anything I would ever wish on my worst enemy, but it's my story, and it showed me early on that God was right there all along.

When I was abused, God was there in my heart, giving me hope for a better future. When I got married at sixteen, God was right there, even though it felt like my world was turning upside down. When I grew up and still faced abuse from friends and family, God was there with his hands on my shoulders, imparting his immense wisdom, gentle kindness, and Endless Love.

You have faced problems and circumstances in your life far different from my own. But God was there for you, too. Even if you have a hard time believing it, it's as true for you as it was for me. God is the alpha and omega, the beginning and the end, and His love is dependable and enduring through any storm in life. It should comfort you to know He will never abandon you, never forget you, and will always love you. His love is beyond anything we can truly imagine, but God tells us in his word in 1 Corinthians chapter 13: verses 4-7:

> *Love is patient and kind; love does not envy or boast; it is not arrogant or rude. It does not insist on its own way; it is not irritable or resentful; it does not rejoice at wrongdoing but rejoices with the truth. Love bears all things, believes all things, hopes all things, endures all things. [1Co 13:4-7 ESV]*

This type of love is not easily found. Every human being desires this deep love. But to receive love, we must first learn how to give it back. This is a substantial challenge, but also a gift we can open at any time. If we grow in our love for God, we naturally learn how to love ourselves and love others. Loving God is the starting point to endless, countless, and infinite love.

AGÁPE LOVE

The English language does a terrible job of defining "love." The word "love" doesn't always accurately convey the right meaning in the right context. I can think of many things I "love:"

- I "love" God.

- I "love" learning new things.

- I "love" eating healthy and exercising.

- I "love" technology.

- I "love" music.

- I "love" my family.

- I "love" fashion.

- I "love" science.

"Love" is defined differently in each unique situation. I don't love music nearly as much as I love my family, and I have a major passion for fashion. The English word love doesn't do a good job of differentiating and defining what love really means. And the more you "love" something or someone, the more you wish there were other words to describe just how much love you feel!

Agápe (pronounced ah-gah-pahy) is one Greek word for love. Two other words for love: Philautia love (self-love), and philia love (love for others) we will cover in the next two chapters to view love from a variety of angles. Agápe love means an empathetic and universal love for all. It's the best word we have for describing what God's love is and what it looks like. According to the New World Encyclopedia:[3]

In the New Testament, however, agápe was frequently used to mean something more distinctive: the unconditional, self-sacrificing, and volitional love of God for humans through Jesus, which they ought also to reciprocate by practicing Agápe love towards God and among themselves.

---

[3] "Agape." New World Encyclopedia, . 7 Feb 2019, 15:57 UTC. 15 Dec 2021, 12:52 <https://www.newworldencyclopedia.org/p/index.php?title=Agape&oldid=1017946>.

Agápe love, simply put, is the awesome and never-ending love God has for us. He loves us unconditionally and without question. Even though the fall of man in the Garden of Eden separated us from Him, He showed his never-ending love. With the death of His son Jesus, He atoned for our sin so that we may never again be separated from Him. Never again, as in forever and for all time. There is no greater love because no greater love could exist.

The Bible further expands on this ever-present love:

> *Can anything ever separate us from Christ's love? Does it mean he no longer loves us if we have trouble or calamity, or are persecuted, or hungry, or destitute, or in danger, or threatened with death? ... No, despite all these things, overwhelming victory is ours through Christ, who loved us. And I am convinced that nothing can ever separate us from God's love. Neither death nor life, neither angels nor demons, neither our fears for today nor our worries about tomorrow--not even the powers of hell can separate us from God's love. No power in the sky above or in the earth below--indeed, nothing in all creation will ever be able to separate us from the love of God that is revealed in Christ Jesus our Lord. [Rom 8:35, 37-39 NLT]*

Loving with Agápe love is the ideal, and the goal we should aim for. Doing so means loving and expecting nothing in return.

This unconditional love is hard to put into action because we are naturally selfish creatures. It's a constant battle of loving others even when they don't deserve it. We can never fully love like God but attempting to do so will bring us closer to Him, closer to ourselves, and closer to others.

Agápe love is the perfect love that God has for us, but that doesn't mean perfection is the end goal. When God said, "And you shall love the Lord your God with all your heart, and with all your soul, and with all your mind, and with all your strength." He did not mean for us to get it right 100% of the time. We are to love Him to the best of our ability, even if that means we fail more than we succeed.

In our current Earthly bodies, we are finite beings who need to work, eat, sleep, take care of others, and take care of ourselves. God does not expect us to kneel in prayer sixteen hours per day, nor does He want us to ignore Him altogether when life gets busy. Reaching a balance of life and love is key, and something you must find and determine for yourself. Start by getting on your knees and asking God to help you love. This simple practice is the best way to begin.

SEVEN BASIC DISCIPLINES FOR PUTTING GOD FIRST

No matter where you're at in your journey, I want to help you along. I want you to meet and commune with God. I want you to begin to understand Agápe love and know just how special it is that God loves us. It's so indescribable it's hard to put into words, but as you experience the deep love God has for you, you can't help but be kinder to yourself and to others. The world becomes a place where you can give back, not a place with danger lurking around every corner. Instead of perilous challenges, you will find opportunity. This truth has changed my life, and I can't wait for you to discover it for yourself.

Here are seven basic spiritual disciplines designed to bring you closer to God and to open up your heart to His love:

1. Pray wherever you are.

2. Make prayer a habit, morning, evening, mealtimes, etc.

3. Schedule time to be in God's word.

4. Practice mindfulness and meditation in order to become more self-aware.

5. Fast from food, social media, entertainment, etc.

6. Fellowship with other believers.

7. Live out your faith by seeing and answering a need around you.

1) PRAY WHEREVER YOU ARE

I love the LORD because he hears my voice and my prayer for mercy. Because he bends down to listen, I will pray as long as I have breath! [Psalm 116:1-2 NLT]

Surrendering to God in a posture of prayer is the easiest spiritual discipline to master. You don't have to speak fancy words or know exactly what to say. Falling to your knees in prayer is the way to start the conversation and develop intimacy with God. If you can't sit on your knees (I know not everyone reading this is a spring chicken!) sit in a lotus position or a special chair in your home reserved for prayer. However, you do it, the point is to make it special, not to hurt yourself or be super uncomfortable.

When I was struggling to cope with abuse after abuse after abuse, I got on my knees and asked God to help me. I knew why I was so broken and could no longer live the same way, but I didn't know how to fix myself. I was ready for change. I was ready for God to make his way into my heart and shine His light. I was ready for a new beginning, and it started the moment I surrendered in my heart. I didn't know what to do next, but He did.

If you aren't sure how to begin, start with the following brief prayer as you quiet your mind:

Lord, I am here. God, grant me direction, wisdom, and the peace that passes all understanding. Speak to me. Fill my heart with compassion for the lost and the lonely. Show me what you want me to do. Fill me with your love so that I might show it to others. Help me out of my troubles. Heal my body and mind. Help me focus today on the things that are pleasing to you. Keep me from sin and lead me to right action. Be with me and guide my steps in all that I do. Stay with me in my time of need. Don't go away, stay right here. Amen!

2) MAKE PRAYER A HABIT, MORNING, EVENING, MEALTIMES, ETC.

Prayer should be a regular part of your walk with God. It's less about doing the task just to cross it off a list, and more to do with opening your heart to God. It doesn't have to be long or a thirty-minute ceremony. I start my day with prayer, and I pray internally throughout the day. Sometimes I just give thanks for life and thanks for the trees that give oxygen or for the healing rays of the sun. Some days I just thank God for his beauty on the earth. Prayer is like talking to your best friend throughout the day.

Pray as you brush your teeth, on your drive before turning on the radio, over your coffee as you blow upon the steam to cool it down, or right before you go into a stressful afternoon meeting. Prayer habits ensure regular communication with God and make sure you are always ready to hear from Him.

I used to go weeks at a time without ever uttering a prayer to God. It's normal to ebb and flow in your spiritual discipline practice. Nobody gets it right all the time, so don't feel bad if this is your current struggle. The key is to become self-aware, know you are not talking to God often enough, and then to decide to do something about it. Working in regular times to talk to God means you won't forget or let too much time go by without stopping to hear from Him.

Start by making prayer or meditation a habit at certain times a day, and then speak to God at various times throughout your day. The best thing about prayer is that you don't need to understand how it works, you just need to be open to talking to God and then listening to what He has to say.

3) SCHEDULE TIME TO BE IN GOD'S WORD

Donald S. Whitney in his book, *Spiritual Disciplines for the Christian Life*, shares his hardcore and relentless approach to scheduling time to be in God's word.

> *"No Spiritual Discipline is more important than the intake of God's Word. Nothing can substitute for it. There simply is no healthy Christian life apart from a diet of the milk and meat of Scripture. The reasons for this are obvious. In the Bible, God tells us about Himself, and especially about Jesus Christ, the incarnation of God. The Bible unfolds the Law of God to us and shows us how we've all broken it. There we learn how Christ died as a sinless, willing Substitute for breakers of God's Law and how we must repent and believe in Him to be right with God. In the Bible, we learn the ways and will of the Lord. We find in Scripture how God wants us to live, and what brings the most joy and satisfaction in life. None of this eternally essential information can be found anywhere else except the Bible. Therefore, if we would know God and be godly, we must know the Word of God—intimately."*
>
> **—Donald S. Whitney**[4]

One key to putting God first is intentionality. This means purposefully planning your schedule to include moments to sit

---

[4] Whitney, Donald, and J. Packer I. Spiritual Disciplines for the Christian Life. Enlarged-Revised, NavPress, 2014.

with God in silence, pray your heart out, and read from His word. I've found that God speaks in a still, small voice ensuring our full attention. God doesn't shout across the room for us to hear Him, He prefers we be ready to hear His words. God not only speaks to us through sound but also in silence. There are so many mysteries of Him throughout the universe. During the darkest times of my life I have heard His voice through nature or a stranger.

Silent time with God doesn't mean you have to lock yourself in a closet. You can have quiet time with God on an evening walk, on your commute with the radio turned off, or on your lunch break. Location matters less than your attention. Come to God wherever and whenever. Schedule time in your calendar to spend time with God.

4) PRACTICE MINDFULNESS AND MEDITATION IN ORDER TO BECOME MORE SELF-AWARE

Growing in self-awareness and knowing how you are doing (not just how you think you are doing) is a great way to start practicing Endless Love toward God, yourself, and others. There are infinite distractions in our daily lives, but our own negative and erroneous thoughts will lead us astray if we aren't careful.

Mindfulness and meditation are excellent for taking an outside view of your life. Learning to see yourself how God sees you starts with becoming more aware of your surroundings and the perspectives of other people. I start every day with meditation and prayer. This primes my mind, my heart, and my soul to embrace the day ahead for what it is. It gives me the power to manifest a positive and productive day because I am building resilience in my mind to better cope with whatever life throws at me.

Let God show you how to think, not the world. Let God be your conscience that guides you. Be careful of input from popular shows and even books or news. Be intentional about what you put inside your brain. The world tells us we aren't good enough. God tells us He loves us no matter what. The world says we need XYZ, but God says we need Him. The world might laugh at us, ridicule us, or even spit on us, but God cherishes and delights in our presence.

Start with just a few minutes every morning. Before you fully wake and dive into your day, spend time in silence. Take several deep breaths and broaden your focus. Don't think about specifics for the day yet. Just sit and give your mind the freedom it so desperately needs.

Mindfulness and meditation lead to an increased ability to see yourself and the world through the eyes of God. It should put a smile on your face to know that you are loved, and that there is nothing you can do that separates you from God's love. Knowing this truth, thinking about it throughout your day, and meditating on it will arm you for the battlefield that is normal life.

5) FAST FROM FOOD, SOCIAL MEDIA, ENTERTAINMENT, ETC.

Fasting is a discipline many want to ignore, but I wouldn't recommend leaving it out. Not only is regular fasting from food good for your health,[5] it's a potent way to break away from the constant need for food by replacing it with other disciplines. Waiting to eat breakfast until later in the day or eliminating late night snacking habits significantly increases the time you can spend doing other things.

Try intermittent fasting from food and see if you like it (eating for eight hours and fasting for sixteen or eating normally for five days of the week and fasting the other two). Go a week without looking at any form of social media or news. Cancel Netflix or wait a week before you binge-watch the next episodes of your favorite show. The spiritual discipline of fasting is all about taking time away from the things of the world and replacing them with nourishment from the Lord via prayer, time in his word, or being still and listening for Him to speak to you.

For beginners I recommend removing a food you enjoy from your diet for three days (ex. meat, cake, cookies, latte; etc.). For the three days avoid the food you removed, set specific times to pray, identify a scripture or affirmation to meditate on and avoid social events. During your fasting it's important to be mindful of your conversations and your activities. Spiritual fasting is a

---

[5] De Cabo R and Mattson MP. Effects of intermittent fasting on health, aging, and disease. New England Journal of Medicine. 2019;381(26):2541-2551. doi: 10.1056/NEJMra1905136.

powerful way to manifest breakthroughs in your life. To learn more about this topic I recommend: The Power of Prayer and fasting Dr Myles Munroe.

6) FELLOWSHIP WITH OTHER BELIEVERS

Prioritize time with other believers to grow spiritually. Church is a natural avenue for this discipline, but doing a Bible study with friends, inviting believing family members over for dinner, or serving your community with fellow believers works too.

Time spent in the real world doing good works is the best way to experience spiritual growth as a team. Putting shoe boxes together for less fortunate is one way to grow together in faith with fellow believers and keep our cups filled. Some of the best fellowship you will experience comes when serving those in need with fellow believers.

Learn from people strong in the faith, but never forget you are there to influence, encourage, motivate, and inspire others as well. Living in a bubble is not what I am suggesting. Lead those around you to good works and surround yourself with people willing to do what needs to be done to help the community.

7) LIVE OUT YOUR FAITH BY SEEING AND ANSWERING A NEED AROUND YOU

God wants us to practice our spirituality. We must take action and be the light! I believe this is the most often neglected spiritual discipline. The book of James Chapter 2 verses 14-17 help to illustrate why service is so important:

> *What good is it, my brothers, if someone says he has faith but does not have works? Can that faith save him? If a brother or sister is poorly clothed and lacking in daily food, and one of you says to them, "Go in peace, be warmed and filled," without giving them the things needed for the body, what good is that? So also, faith by itself if it does not have works, is dead. [Jas 2:14-17 ESV]*

If we have faith and believe, and yet we don't practice application, are we really any better than an unbeliever? I take passages like this to heart, so that when I see someone who is hungry and desperately yearning for attention and love, I answer. And further, the very fact that I answer these calls from God in the first place has helped to establish my belief that we must go out and serve others.

When you see the surrounding need, act. There is no better way to practice the spiritual discipline of living out your faith.

RISING TO THE TASK

I used to walk by Mike every day on my way to pick up lunch. The world, in all its wisdom, says to ignore the homeless to not make the problem worse, but is this really the best approach? After what felt like the millionth time walking by Mike, I stopped walking and asked him to lunch. I heard a still soft voice say, "buy him lunch and ask him if he would like to talk", so I did. It was incredibly uncomfortable, but I did it anyway. While grabbing sandwiches at a local deli in Downtown D.C., I learned a lot about Mike, as he was kind enough to share his story with me.

"I was just like you and everyone else that passes by me every day." He told me. "I got tired, so I took all of my money out of the bank, got on a bus, and came to D.C. I'm from Ohio and I had a decent job making good money, but I just didn't want to work anymore, and I decided to make a change. All my basic needs are met. People always come the same way you did. "God will always send someone."

I thought I was helping Mike, but Mike helped me see the world differently. I learned that you can't judge a book by its cover. You never know where life is going to take you. I looked forward to having lunch with him the few times we could. I remember looking for Mike during lunch time and all I found was his lifeless body on the ground. Mike passed away from natural causes.

I'm glad now that I was obedient, and I took the time to get to know this man. He was humble, and he had love in his heart. I don't know if he had children or had ever been married, but I will never forget the frail, soft-spoken white guy that would sit at the L'Enfant Plaza metro station.

You never know what a person has gone through. Your life can change instantly. You can be up today and down tomorrow. Each of us has a story to tell. Maybe Mike just didn't have the strength to continue his day-to-day life, or maybe something traumatic happened to him. I'll never know. Hearing his story and feeling like I was actually helping this man filled my heart with the utmost of joy.

But of course, not everyone agreed with my actions...

After finishing another fun and interesting lunch with Mike, an elderly lady stopped me to give me a piece of her mind. She said, "You're the problem, you know?"

Her statement took me aback, and I responded with, "Excuse me, what are you talking about?"

She pointed first to me and then to Mike as she said, "It's because of people like *you* we have people like *that* on the street." She hurried away without another word.

I tried not to let the moment bother me, but of course it got my wheels turning. Was I doing the right thing? I'm not ignorant of the harsh reality of life on the streets. It's because I know how tough it can be that my heart cried out for Mike. I knew money wouldn't make a major difference, and might even make things worse, but lunch and a friend? How could my actions be wrong?

Putting God first means obeying him. When God tells you to do something, even if it's contrary to what others want or expect from you, it's your duty to follow that call. It's never easy, but once you practice it, you'll get better at following God's heart for your life. God desires for us to desire Him, and we learn to desire Him by following his call. Always be mindful Gods voice has no sin in it. God will never

Having lunch with Mike meant putting God first and doing what He asks of me, regardless of how I or other people feel or think. Learning to put God first means quieting the inner voice of selfish desires and listening to your growing heart. Spiritual growth occurs when we do the thing that scares us, only to find it more fulfilling than we could have ever imagined.

Learning basic spiritual disciplines is merely the beginning of the journey. Living out agápe love takes years of practice, but success or failure isn't something you can track on a whiteboard or spreadsheet. The sign that you are internalizing and comprehending the concept of agápe love is when you do things for others that might be considered by the majority to be unsafe or unwise, but you can't help but listen to the call of your heart! These are the moments you should be proud of, even if other people look down at you with scorn or confusion. We don't know who we pass by every day. Everyone has a story.

As you dive deeper into Endless Love, remember the enormous pull of God's love. He is always waiting, always watching, and always expecting you to return to Him. When you listen to His call, you are safe, even if everything is falling apart. No matter what is happening in your life right now, God has you in His arms. Trust. Keep working. Don't quit. Keep growing closer to Him.

PRACTICING ENDLESS LOVE

- **Pray:** *Lord, show me how to love you. Teach me how you want me to grow in spiritual discipline. Help me learn and practice the things you want me to do. Use me to advance your kingdom. Help me to learn how to love you, myself, and others at the incredible and awesome level that you love us! Let me drink in your love and let it fill my heart with compassion, patience, and clarity of purpose. Give me wisdom and strength as I take on today. Bless all those around me and lead me to be a blessing in my own way. Amen!*

- **Read:** If you love reading, or are hoping to cultivate a great new habit, start a reading list. Then be intentional about actually reading the books on the list. The book, *Battlefield of the Mind: Winning the Battle in Your Mind* by New York Times bestselling author Joyce Meyer, is a must-read book. As you seek God first, forces threatening to control your mind will challenge you. Be resilient and win the battle! ***Pro reader's tip, always check your local library for books before purchasing! And, if you want a sample of the book before reading, you can often download part of the eBook version to read a few pages to test the waters.**

- **Act:** Practice Endless Love first thing in the morning. If you truly desire to grow in your relationship with God, put him first. Practice prayer, read scripture, recite an affirmation, or watch a short devotional video before you do anything else to start your day. If you struggle to add new habits into your routine, try stacking this new habit with an old one, like brushing your teeth or making breakfast. We are creatures of habit for sure, but we can use this for our own good by forming new positive habits that change our lives.

CHAPTER TWO
PASSIONATELY AND INTENTIONALLY LOVING YOURSELF

"Love brings you face to face with yourself, It's impossible to love others if you don't love yourself" by John Pierrkos

Roughly 10 million Americans per year suffer some form of abuse.[6] As I've alluded to, I've had to experience this nightmare. You may have suffered abuse of some sort in your life. It's still far too common. If you're going through abuse, please get help. Don't wait. You deserve love. If you've gone through it and are recovering, know that you are not alone. What happened to you does not need to define you. What others say you are is nothing compared to who God says you are! Rest in that truth.

---

[6] "National Statistics". NCADV. National Coalition Against Domestic Violence. Retrieved 5 October 2018.

My journey has been fraught with difficulty and hardship. But I realized I didn't have a personal cheerleading team pushing me towards my goals. If I wanted peace, happiness or joy, that meant I was going to be my own motivation. I've done a lot of work to overcome and to learn to love myself, but it's taken time and effort to do so. It's been hard, but this journey granted me resilience and keen insight. I eventually broke the cycle and learned to love myself for who I was, and this shift changed my life.

Early into adulthood, I gave of myself freely, without too much concern or awareness for how I was doing. I put others first, but without boundaries, I was losing myself. I learned the hard way that you can't authentically love anyone if you don't intentionally love yourself. If you don't have admiration and passion for your mind, your body, and your life, it's difficult to show love to anyone else, especially in the long run.

After focusing on God and learning to love Him, the next step is loving oneself. In order to give love, you need to first embrace it in your own heart and then give it to your own heart. You must take care of your own needs first before you're able to help others. Just like they always say to put on your own oxygen mask before helping someone else, your ability and capacity to love others is directly tied to your personal strength. You can't give what you don't have. This quote from the late actress Lucille Ball further illustrates the point:

> *Love yourself first and everything falls into line. You really have to love yourself to get anything done in this world.*

I found myself, on many occasions, giving and doing for others out of pure obligation and not from a place of love. I was serving my family and friends by fulfilling every need they had and leaving no room for myself. It didn't matter how I felt, just that others were happy, pleased, and/or satisfied. Even if I snuck into the bathroom to cry after a particularly difficult crisis, at least everyone else was doing okay. Who was I to complain? The people around me were happy, so that's all that mattered... Right? Wrong.

Many of us live our lives trying to please others. After a while it becomes difficult to keep up with the demands of others. I have learned if you put out people will always remain to receive. But the moment you decide to choose you and deny others, it may upset your friends and family, because they are accustomed to you being available when they need you.

When I started to take more time to discover me it meant I had to deny others. It was difficult at first, but it was necessary for my healing. It takes time to discover who you are and what makes you significant. You should never apologize for loving yourself and taking care of you. I do understand there will be times when you must make sacrifices to help others but there should always be a healthy balance. If you find yourself over-whelmed, filled with anxiety, and stressed while helping others or just doing life stop, slow down and reevaluate what you're doing and why you're doing it.

We live in a society where we're led to believe the faster the better. Better for who? Taking time to love you means taking time to learn you. Be patient with yourself and take to intimately discover you. Don't allow others to fill your day with unfilled errands and activities that benefit them. You must learn to avoid activities and things that no longer serve you and make you better. Put your energy in to creating a better version of you.

FILL YOUR CUP

Keeping your own cup topped off and your energy levels stocked is how you keep giving to others at a high level. I used to overlook myself and ignore the complete lack of peace I had serving others. My heart just wasn't in it anymore. It's not that I didn't want to serve them, I just couldn't give at the high level I was giving. I constantly made myself available to others, even if that meant denying my own basic needs. You can't pour from an empty cup, but I was doing it, anyway. I was completely drained and utterly exhausted, but I kept giving. My pace was unsustainable, and I knew it. I started noticing how much this was affecting my health, my mind, and my relationship with God. I didn't like that I was becoming a shell of my former self and I knew I needed a change.

I had a major problem with saying *no*, even when answering *yes* felt like a prison sentence. I knew in my heart and my head that *no* was the right answer, but my lips said *yes* out of habit. I was giving more than I could, (emotionally and mentally) and at a higher capacity than I could handle. Secret emotional break-downs and frequent mood swings were the norm.

God is selfless, but we are not God. Jesus gave all he had to others, but he had quite a lot to give! We are absolutely fooling ourselves if we think we can get away with neglecting to fill our own cup and not recharging our batteries from time to time. Scripture tells us directly that the first step is learning to love God, and the second is to love others **as we love ourselves:**

> *And he answered, "You shall love the Lord your God with all your heart and with all your soul and with all your strength and with all your mind, **and your neighbor as yourself.**" [Luke 10:27 ESV, emphasis mine]*

It leaves us with a poignant question, how can I possibly love others if I don't first understand and incorporate love for myself into my heart? The answer is you can't, not fully. Love for others must follow the love we have for God and the love we have for ourselves.

PHILAUTIA: SELF-LOVE

Similar to our previous discussion on the word "agápe," philautia is another Greek word for love. Philautia specially means "self-love," and it involves looking deep into your soul and finding nothing but joy and contentment for who you are. It's showing yourself love even when no one else will. It's valuing yourself enough to take care of your own needs so that you can be in it for the long haul.

Some definitions go on to extend the meaning to, "promoting the self over all others, both brother and father, neighbor and God."[7] For obvious reasons, we don't go this far with our definition. Certainly, I don't mean to say we should put ourselves above other people and/or God Himself! Philautia is just one aspect of love. On it's own it could be self-fulfilling and selfish, but together, with the other types of love, it's an essential part of Endless Love.

Philautia love means saying no to the needs of others and focusing on yourself. When I was finally learning the power of saying no, I was living a hectic lifestyle with family, a full-time job, and other obligations. I knew loaning the money to a friend or time spent over the weekend to fill a family need was adding more to my plate than I could chew, but I did it anyway. I wanted to make sure they weren't mad at me and would accept me, so

---

[7] "philautia" – WordSense Online Dictionary (15th December, 2021) <https://www.wordsense.cu/philautia/>

yes became my go-to response. I said *yes* without considering the consequences.

I eventually arrived at a moment in time where life was becoming unbearable and miserable. I was losing myself to family, friends, and work. Saying no was hard for me, but I knew it was necessary to prioritize my own needs. People didn't seem to care and would relentlessly ask me to do things for them. All they wanted was for me to say *yes* and take care of their needs, regardless of what it might do to me.

I sometimes wondered if they (or anybody!) cared that I was suffering too. I felt numb, and I disliked the person I was becoming; someone with resentful thoughts towards others. Frequently, people would insist on my help without considering the heavy load I already had. I noticed how mean people were when I didn't agree with them or when I didn't let their problem become my priority. It was the same individuals with the same sob stories over and over again.

I finally realized that other people were blocking me from the self-love I deserved, the self-love that God desired for me to have! Practicing the love of philautia toward myself felt like a completely foreign concept, but as soon as I began, I unlocked a whole new world. I soon realized I was truly lacking in this area, and that if I could get it right, I would be better able to serve others! It was an eye-opening revelation that had been staring me right in the face.

We think we must give 100% of ourselves, 100% of the time, but this is an impossible expectation we place on ourselves, and not what God intended. We are beings with limited resources, and we must be practical and intentional about how we use these gifts. We must practice philautia love. We cannot be all things, for all people, all the time.

SELF-LOVE IS NOT SELFISH

To love oneself is the beginning of a life-long romance.

— **Oscar Wilde**

Most of the hurt I experienced growing up and into adulthood was by those closest to me. I realized I had a choice whether to open myself up to my family. I realized it's not a requirement to continue to have close relationships with certain people, former friends, or family members, just because they are familiar relationships! I realized who was for me and who wasn't by analyzing how they would respond to my failures and my successes. When I would leave the presence of specific people feeling heavy, hurt, and empty, I knew it was time to make a change. As I prayed and asked God for healing, He gave me peace to walk away from certain relationships and move on. It's not selfish, it's self-love, and it's vital.

Some people can't go along with where God is taking you. Unfortunately, certain people might even block you from achieving growth. They may not understand the gift or purpose inside you. Not everyone will be for you or will push you toward your destiny. Some people will hold on for dear life trying to keep you in the valley with them. It's not selfish to move on by telling these types of people no.

There is a fine line between selfishness and self-love. I want to be cognizant of the difference. I'm not suggesting selfishness or putting oneself first at the neglect of all others. What I'm saying is that we get this wrong far too often. Our culture focuses too heavily on the self and personal needs over the needs of all, and this isn't good either. I propose we strike a balance lest the pendulum swings too far to either side.

> *Self-Love is not selfish; you cannot truly love another until you know how to love yourself.*
>
> — **Author Unknown**

It's not selfish to love yourself. It's wise to focus on yourself and what is going on in your life. Just like agápe love, mastering philautia love is important, but not to the exclusion of the other forms of love. If you ONLY lived for yourself and philautia love was all you practiced, you would likely become a self-interested and selfish hermit. You may even deny all need of God and reject society altogether. This would not be Endless Love.

Loving yourself is keeping your cup of steaming hot cocoa full, so you always have the capacity to share with others at a high level. It's learning to meet your own needs first so you can give back to others, but also fall in love with yourself! You are unique, and wonderful, and lovely, but you need to step back and give yourself a chance to believe it. I've never met you, and I firmly believe you are deserving of much love.

You are more than enough, just as you are. God loves you exactly as you are, but He loves you far too much to let you stay there. He will accept you and take you in wherever you are, but He wants you to grow closer to Him. Growing closer to God and loving yourself more deeply means seriously looking at your current abilities, needs, circumstances, strengths, etc. It means becoming more self-aware and asking really annoying and painful questions to drag yourself out of any mud holding you back.

Let me ask you three tough questions. Stop and reflect honestly. Don't skip these questions, especially if they seem painful. Pain brings change, so don't be afraid to think deeply and then act:

1. Do I truly love myself?

2. Do I have a problem with myself?

3. Do I love every part of me, including the parts of my body I don't really like or would prefer to change?

Before you continue, reflect. Let the truth sink in for a moment. There is no judgment intended by this author, and I don't want you to judge yourself too harshly. Instead, note any thoughts that surface and face them honestly. You can only learn to love yourself if you realize there's work to be done. It's hard to tackle these deeper issues and face yourself, but it's worth the time and effort to reflect and then take action.

SEVEN WAYS TO SHOW LOVE TO YOURSELF

I have decided to stick to love; hate is too great a burden to bear.

— Martin Luther King, Jr.

After you take the time to reflect on your own capacity to love, take action on that self-love. Practice one or all of these seven strategies for loving yourself and living out philautia love:

1. Spend time alone.

2. Look deep within.

3. Guard your time, learn to say no.

4. Treat your body right.

5. Don't cover up shame, embrace it and deal with it.

6. Stop comparing yourself to others.

7. Turn off the world's view of you and embrace who God says you are.

Mastery of all seven of these approaches isn't necessary. I am still far from perfect at balancing it all. We're all learning and growing and that includes you, too. The key is to note what resonates with you as you learn. And remember, loving yourself is just one part of the bigger picture. Learn to grow in love with who God made you to be, and then get busy taking action.

1) SPEND TIME ALONE

If you have a problem being alone and spending time with yourself, there may be a deeper problem. Spending time alone is how you learn to listen to the positive voice inside your head. It's how you hear your own thoughts! Many busybodies and people who never seem to stop can't face themselves alone. They don't even stop to look in the mirror because they don't want to face the reflection staring back at them. Does that sound like your present self?

Stop searching for "true love" and words of affirmation from other people. True love starts with self-love and understanding who you are. When you're ready, love will find you. This is not merely a fancy cliche. It's true! If your heart is pure, open and ready, love will find its way to you because you are welcoming it into your life. If you practice self-love first, you will draw people to you who are ready to show you love in the way you need it.

It can take a lifetime to discover who you truly are, especially if you don't stop and make the time to do so! If you come from a family that dictated and controlled your life, it will be challenging and scary when it's time for you to go it alone. Life will challenge you with many obstacles. Sometimes you may have to face these obstacles without help from others. You will always have God but being alone and without help here on Earth can be a major struggle.

Free time used to be hard for me. Whenever I had time on my hands, my first thought was who could I call and who could I hang out with? I never thought of spending that time alone. I wanted to distract myself from thoughts about me and my life by being with other people. I convinced myself I was doing it for them, but strangely, hanging out with others when I should have spent time alone was the most selfish thing I could have done.

Spending time with just me, and actually learning to enjoy it, took time. It was a laborious process to master and didn't happen overnight. But when I finally stopped making myself busy, and instead took the time for myself, my outlook on life changed. I enjoyed, for the first time, the time I spent alone.

Of course, not everyone has the capability to enjoy an abundance of alone time. You might have a demanding job, a full house, or a rigorous schedule of hobbies and activities. If so, that's okay. Do what you can to find time to spend alone:

- Take five minutes before bed and kneel in prayer and/or thought.
- Walk whenever and wherever possible by yourself.

- Be intentional and make time for yourself on your calendar, even if it's just thirty minutes. Skip lunch with a friend if you feel your cup emptying.

- Wake up earlier or go to bed slightly later. Don't lose out on too much sleep but use this newfound time to be alone.

- Appreciate brief moments of solitude and try not to fill them with busy activities. Instead, embrace the opportunity for quiet reflection and time with God.

2) LOOK DEEP WITHIN

For many years, I wasn't taking care of myself, and I was overwhelmed by all the stuff I had going on. It wasn't until circumstances forced alone time upon me (because no one was available) that I finally looked at myself and my issues. I analyzed what was truly robbing me from having a better quality of life. I looked deep within. I didn't like what I found...

Take the time to look deep within to confront your own issues. What you find might scare the heck out of you, but I implore you to do it now, before the darkness gets even worse.

Facing yourself is never fun, but it leads to healing and self-love. As you learn to take more time for alone time, deep reflection will eventually occur. You can speed it along by limiting distractions during alone time. There have to be moments of quietness, peace and restoration, or you won't get where God wants you to go as fast as God wants you to get there.

The process of deep introspection was extremely difficult because I had to face myself. I had to look at who Angela was, and I had to accept myself; all truths, all pains, all fake realities, everything. The truth hurts, and it's difficult to deal with it. But whose fault is that, really? If it gets to the point where it scares you to look too deep within, you've been on the highway far too long without taking the exit. Take the exit! Get off the highway of runaway negativity. Face your issues with a grim resolve full of love and patience. Don't be hard on yourself. Instead, love yourself enough to open the doors to healing.

3) GUARD YOUR TIME, LEARN TO SAY NO

Discover just how much love you have to give by reducing stress and overwhelm. When others ask you to do something for them or with them, say no if you need to. Determining when and how to say no takes time, but guarding your time is important for loving yourself. If you say yes to everything, you'll have no time for God, no time for yourself, and ultimately, no time for others. Time is the one currency that is equal for all of us. Nobody has any more or any less of it than anybody else. There are twenty-four hours in a day and even the most productive can't get around this truth.

Love requires an investment of time. Say no to things, people, events, and opportunities that don't fit into your life right now so you can fall in love with yourself. The best way to begin is to lean on the side of no by saying no to most new opportunities. Exercise your no muscle and build margin into your life. Don't feel bad saying no. Instead, enjoy your newly gained free time.

4) TREAT YOUR BODY RIGHT

Eat right. Get enough sleep. Exercise often. The importance of practicing these three essential habits has been told to you all of your life. Well, here's one more time because it's so important, and it's always useful to read reminders like these. The foods you eat and the things you do directly affect your happiness and the way you think. Here are three ways to keep feeling like a spring chicken no matter how old you get:

- **Be mindful about what foods you put into your body.** Quality counts when considering what foods to eat.[8] Focus on adding fruits and vegetables into your diet and you'll be well on your way to taking care of your body. Practice healthy eating by purchasing new and exciting fruits and vegetables, and then searching for new recipes. It doesn't have to be complicated, and it's not a lack of new ideas preventing you from getting serious about eating healthy. What's stopping you is that you might feel okay now and aren't motivated for change but be cognizant that everything we put into our bodies is affecting us in some way. Make the food you eat count in positive ways that gives you energy and doesn't create hidden diseases you have to deal with later on.

- **Get the right amount of sleep for you.** In a 2014 survey conducted by the National Sleep Foundation, 35% of American adults rated their quality of sleep as "poor"

---

[8] "The Best Diet: Quality Counts." The Nutrition Source, 15 Mar. 2018, www.hsph.harvard.edu/nutritionsource/healthy-weight/best-diet-quality-counts/#ref23.

or "only fair."[9] What would you rate the quality of your sleep? Could it be better? You can't practice love if you're falling out of your chair in need of a nap every other day. In an article called *Short and Long-Term Health Consequences of Sleep Disruption,*[10] the authors showed that even short-term disruption of sleep led to numerous potential problems including an increased stress response, reduced quality of life, emotional distress, issues with cognition and memory, and even behavioral problems in otherwise healthy individuals. Sleep is a big deal! Make sure you are consistently getting at least seven to eight hours per night for optimal health benefits. If not, make it a priority to find a way that works for you to sleep better and more often. Show yourself love and get to bed!

- **Exercise often.** Walk as often as you can and strength train or practice cardio one to two times per week. A 2006 article in the Canadian Medical Association Journal confirmed that exercise is critical for optimal health, prevention of diseases, and avoidance of premature death.[11] Exercising also makes you feel great mentally

---

[9] National Sleep Foundation. 2014 Sleep Health Index. Arlington, VA: National Sleep Foundation; 2014.

[10] Medic, Goran et al. "Short- and long-term health consequences of sleep disruption." Nature and science of sleep vol. 9 151-161. 19 May. 2017, doi:10.2147/NSS.S134864

[11] Warburton, Darren E R et al. "Health benefits of physical activity: the evidence." CMAJ : Canadian Medical Association journal = journal de l'Association medicale canadienne vol. 174,6 (2006): 801-9. doi:10.1503/cmaj.051351

and physically. Exercise can shift just about any bad mood to a positive one and can change your outlook in a tough situation. Don't skip exercise, even if it's just ten minutes of walking per day.

Treat your body right so that you can be in it for the long haul. Be an example to your kids, your friends, and your family of what it means to take care of yourself. Do right by your body and show love to your earthly temple.

5) DON'T COVER UP SHAME, EMBRACE IT AND DEAL WITH IT

I used to wear my shame like a coat of colors. I dressed it up with my flashy jewelry, designer clothes, flashy cars, and pricey handbags. This was me, except it wasn't me at all. Shame was all around me; ever present in everything I put to the forefront of what people saw. But of course, it was all fake. This facade of shame was blocking me from becoming who I really wanted to be.

This is what I know: Today, I am free from fear, intimidation, lack of resources, lack of understanding, and lack of faith. I lack nothing, for I have God. I am a new creature. I am the woman God has created me to be. I am not who or what man says I am. I am not limited by the standards of this world, but I know I have been created for such a time as this. I will not stop becoming, and I will not be ashamed of my past.

Don't let shame stop you from becoming exactly who God made you to be. We all mess up. We all have issues. Shame says you couldn't possibly measure up, that everything you are is not enough. I am shouting at you from these pages that this just isn't true! Your shame doesn't define you. You have nothing to be ashamed of! Let God wash it all away and show you just how amazing and irreplaceable you are. Shame has no hold over you. Throw it off like a coat and enter into the new freedom of self-love.

6) STOP COMPARING YOURSELF TO OTHERS

> *For you formed my inward parts; you knitted me together in my mother's womb. I praise you, for I am fearfully and wonderfully made. Wonderful are your works; my soul knows it very well. [Psa 139:13-14 ESV]*

Sometimes you will be the one that sees differently, hears differently, and responds differently than anybody else. People will attack you for being different, family or not. If family or friends don't celebrate your difference, this will cause feelings of confusion, despair, low self-esteem, and intimidation. This can be painful and confusing at the same time and might cause you to wonder why you are different. It might even make you want to change who you are and acclimate instead of embracing your uniqueness.

If you respond in ways others don't expect, it doesn't make you bad, nor does it make you wrong; it makes you different. And this is okay! Celebrate your uniqueness. Standing out amidst a crowd is not a bad thing. Relatives have literally told me I look different from the rest of the family. I didn't understand why I stood out from all the rest or why it mattered at all. I was just being me, and I really like myself! I liked certain styles of music, dressed in my own fashion, and had my own hobbies. They drove out the innocent love for being me, and it happens to kids all the time.

As a young adult, I recall friends saying, "you're so weird..." just because I had a love for adventure. Well, what's wrong with adventure? It didn't make me a bad person, nor was I wrong; it made me different from who I was hanging out with. I had to accept myself and my differences. I've realized through my healing process that each person has that one thing that makes them special. What is special about you? Come on! Don't scoff at this question. Embrace your uniqueness even if it's weird or unpopular.

The thing that makes you special belongs to you. No matter if that thing is making others laugh, your joyful personality, your organization skills, being a good listener, a mediator who seeks harmony, a strong educator, an elegant speaker, etc. No one can duplicate you. Many have tried to duplicate distinguished men and women like Martin Luther King, Corrie Ten Boom,

Michael Jordan, Melinda Gates, Oprah Winfrey, Michael Jackson, etc., but no one can be just like these amazing people.

You are not like anyone else. You are special and unique and perfect in God's sight. Stop negatively comparing yourself to others. It's good, and even healthy, to look up to mentors and to seek what they have, but don't compare your journey to theirs. It might take you years and years to reach a goal that takes someone else only thirty days. So what? Keep working and growing and only compare yourself to yourself.

Always remember that even if it might appear that someone else was an overnight success, this is often a false reality. Behind the scenes of the apparent "overnight success" lies thousands of hours of effort. Work your butt off towards your goals and desires, but don't feel shame or embarrassment when it feels like it's taking forever. Keep on pushing and keep putting the hours in.

7) TURN OFF THE WORLD'S VIEW OF YOU, AND EMBRACE WHO GOD SAYS YOU ARE

> *So, God created man in his own image, in the image of God he created him; male and female he created them.* *[Gen 1:27 ESV]*

God made us in His image. He made YOU in His image. Let that sink in. God, the Creator of the universe and the one above all things, made you and me in His image. He valued us so much that He made us to be like Him. We are so very important to God, even when it feels like no one could love us. It's a truth that doesn't easily penetrate a stubborn mind, and it took many years for me to grasp it. If you don't feel it right away, don't worry. God will fight for you to keep you, but He will never push you away. He will always be exactly what you need.

Unfortunately, the society we operate in values human beings differently from how the Creator values life.

Love yourself through the lens of God, not the lens of the culture and other people. Just like you shouldn't compare yourself to others, don't balk when others stop and stare at you to judge you.

Often, when negativity surfaces, it's other people trying to bring you down to their level and prevent you from taking flight. Don't let their comments take hold! Soar above your potential by embracing who God says you are. Love yourself by remembering God's infinite love for you.

As you practice these seven strategies, find what works for you and refresh your daily habits. Practice self-love so that you can fully become what you are capable of. The more self-love you show yourself, the more you will impact other people and ultimately, bring you and them closer to God.

PRACTICING ENDLESS LOVE

- **Pray:** *Lord, show me how to love myself like you love me. Your love for me is beyond all understanding and my own limited knowledge. I know I need you. I know I need to love myself more than I do. I know I need to set firm boundaries and make space for you to come down and show up in my life. Help me give you the room you need to change me from within. Guide my heart to yours. Help me learn how to love in all of love's plentiful and exciting ways. Amen!*

- **Read:** Read the book *The Power of Positive Thinking* by Norman Vincent Peale. This book will teach you how to believe in who you are. Changing negative thinking is mandatory for growth, but extremely challenging if you were brought up in that type of environment. Read to challenge your way of thinking and to grow a more positive outlook.

- **Act:** Pick one of the seven strategies above for how to love yourself more. Choose one you can implement right now, and take action. Action is the key to making new learning stick. Don't just read and think happy thoughts about what you are "going to do." Instead, take the time to do it today to grow in self-love.

CHAPTER THREE
BOUNDLESS LOVE FOR OTHERS

Having purified your souls by your obedience to the truth for a sincere brotherly love, love one another earnestly from a pure heart. [1Pe 1:22 ESV]

Greater love has no one than this, that someone lay down his life for his friends. [John 15:13 ESV]

t was a terrible day. Work had me bogged down and stressed. The house was a complete disaster, and I just barely made it to school in time to pick up my daughter. I was in a rush, and I'm not afraid to admit that God was far from my mind. It was one of those days you wish you could skip, because nothing would make it better, or so I thought. God has a way of getting your attention when you least expect it, but most need it.

As I picked up my ten-year-old from school, I quickly said "hi," and told her sternly to get her behind in the car, because we were on a tight schedule! I will never forget what she said to me as she settled into the backseat. She looked at me with her big, beautiful eyes and said:

"Mommy, it's okay. You must be having a bad day because you're usually not like this."

I stopped dead in my tracks and quickly checked my attitude. I apologized and thanked her for acknowledging that I wasn't intentionally being mean.

Children can say the darndest things, but I've learned there is infinite wisdom in the mind of a child if we choose to listen carefully. Her simple, yet eloquent words struck a chord in my soul. The more I thought about what she said, the more I wanted to extend others the same amount of grace she extended me at that moment. Everyone has their own secret and even not-so-secret troubles and burdens. What if we all analyzed situations more closely with an eye for grace and forgiveness before we engage with a negative or unhelpful comment? What if we could all be more like my precious daughter at this moment? Wouldn't the world be a much better place if we could extend this grace to everyone?

True love is boundless like the ocean and, swelling within one, spreads itself out and, crossing all boundaries and frontiers, envelops the whole world.

— **Mahatma Gandhi**

Having grace would grant us better outcomes in almost all circumstances. Choosing not to love destroys relationships. Extending grace doesn't mean you're soft or allowing someone else to walk all over you. It simply means you choose to humble yourself to defuse the situation. Love is gentle, love is caring, love is compassionate, and love is attempting to understand others even when the other person is in the wrong. Saying I love you comes easy to many of us, but love is an action word. If you love me today because I made you feel good emotionally, but then hate me tomorrow because of a disagreement, that's not true love, it's false love and deadly to the soul.

Having boundless love for others isn't possible unless you first learn to love God and love yourself. Once you begin the journey toward Endless Love, you will come face to face with the monolith of challenges to becoming a godly person; loving others as yourself. It will take every bit of strength you possess, but loving others will fill your very soul.

PHILIA LOVE

When our community is in a state of peace, it can share that peace with neighboring communities, and so on. When we feel love and kindness towards others, it not only makes others feel loved and cared for, but it helps us also to develop inner happiness and peace.

— Dalai Lama

Philia means brotherly love or close friendship in Greek. It's the last new Greek word you will see in this book, but it's a great way to describe the type of love you have for a close friend, a mentor, a coach, or even a family member you've grown quite close to. Philia love describes a deep love built over years and years of friendship and time spent together. It's plutonic, but it's still deeply important to you.

This is the type of love where you feel you would do anything for the other person. I am lucky to have this type of relationship with my best friend. I met her at work in a business engagement, and we've been side by side ever since. I feel a sense of philia love for her because of the deep connection we have. I would do anything for her and she for me. Philia love results from forming a deep relationship with another person, but it doesn't happen overnight.

It's not the goal for me or for you to have philia love for everyone we meet right off the bat, but you never know if the person standing in your presence could be the answer to your prayers. The random stranger you just met might be someone God intends you to get really close to! It's not possible to know for sure given our limitations and constraints, but it's always a possibility. Some people are only in our lives for a brief time and it might seem impossible to show philia love to them. But we can and should extend people the same grace we would extend to a close friend.

When I am interacting with random strangers at a cafe or losing patience with the receptionist while waiting in line, I try to take a step back and view them as a vitally important person. It doesn't mean I should give all of myself to them or spend the entire day talking to them or supporting them. It means switching to an open mindset and having a willingness to love them, and to love them deeply for however long we might be together. Learning to embrace philia love for all people led me to have lunch with a homeless guy. This openness created an opportunity for invaluable learning and growth on my part. I don't expect that he and I will have the same relationship as me and my best friend, but I still want to be the best person I can be to him and to people like him while I can.

Loving people with a philia love takes practice, and your approach will be different for each person. My friend and I have a very different relationship than me and the homeless guy. It's hard to give someone you don't know the time necessary to build a relationship.

It's much easier to show love to someone you already understand fully. As I've said, I used to go too far and give too much of myself too often. I was trying to love everyone with a philia love right away, and this led to relational burnout. Instead, love others at your capacity and build relationships slowly.

A LANGUAGE OF LOVE

Love is not one size fits all. As we attempt to be more loving to others and to embrace philia love, we will quickly realize how complicated love is. Love has different levels, dimensions, and sounds. Each of us has a different love language (or two) and it's helpful to know how to communicate love to others and how we best receive it ourselves. If we know how others receive and communicate love, their actions will make more sense to us. We might suddenly understand why they do the things they do. Their actions might be born of much more love than we realized, because it was their way of showing love!

In his groundbreaking book, *The Five Love Languages*, Gary Chapman revolutionized the way we think about the language of love.[12] The author shares that we each have a primary way that we receive and feel loved. The five love languages are:

1. **Words of Affirmation:** You appreciate positive and kind words that build you up. You want to hear how well you are doing and how much the other person appreciates you. You feel loved when others verbally tell you how much you mean to them.

2. **Acts of Service:** You feel loved when people take action and take care of things. You believe actions speak louder than words and your heart fills to the brim when

---

[12] Chapman, Gary. The 5 Love Languages: The Secret to Love That Lasts. Reprint, Northfield Publishing, 2015.

someone does the dishes for you, cooks you a nice meal, takes you out on a special date, or drives forty-five minutes out of their way to pick up your dry cleaning.

3. **Receiving Gifts:** You have the love language of receiving gifts if you most feel love when other people give you a gift. Of course, it's not entirely materialistic. It's the idea that they were thinking about you and your needs enough to show it in physical form. Gifts signify to you that the other person was spending their own time thinking about you and this makes you feel an incredible amount of love.

4. **Quality Time:** You value undistracted time spent with people above anything else. You don't care if it's a microwave pizza, a cheap bottle of wine, and a night spent in as long as you get to spend quality time together. When you feel you are the center of attention, the world stops, and you feel loved.

5. **Physical Touch:** If you have the love language of physical touch, you desire intimacy with the other person. This might mean holding hands, hugging, kissing, etc. But this love language isn't purely sexual. If you want to show deeper philia love to other people, it might just mean a hug every time you see them or a hand on their shoulder if they are sharing a personal story.

The approach of the five love languages is just one glimpse into the bigger picture that is human relationships. It's a starting point for practicing Endless Love towards others. It doesn't capture the vastness of uniqueness between various individuals, but it helps paint a clearer picture of the needs of certain people. It's not putting others in a box and placing labels on them but relating to others and showing love starts with understanding them to a higher degree. Once you begin to understand, you can make subtle shifts in your interactions with each person in your life and see how things go. Always start slow and test the waters, but you might just find a simple switch is all you need to unlock a deeper love connection.

If your father-in-law doesn't have the love language of physical touch, you might be better off with a simple handshake and an offer to listen to one of his many stories. If your spouse understands love through quality time, you won't win their affection by doing the dishes or taking out the trash. Instead, leave the dirty dishes out on the counter and take them on a spontaneous walk. If your kids need words of affirmation, be sure to highlight their best attributes as often as possible.

An important piece of the puzzle is to remember that we often give love the same way we receive it. If you are a person whose love language is receiving gifts, it might be the primary way you give love to others because it's all you've known. This can work well, as most people won't turn away gifts, but if the receiver of your gift has *receiving gifts* as their bottom-tier love language, they might appreciate your gift for what it is, but not feel the love you intended. It's important to have a basic understanding of these love languages to ensure you're showing love in a way the specific person understands and will appreciate.

This barrier of differing love languages is one of the primary reasons people struggle in intimate relationships. This mismatch of giving/receiving love in various forms is the essence of why it's so hard to love others.

"But I tell them I love them every day!"

"I spent hours of quality time with them every week!"

"I did the laundry and cleaned the entire house and they still shut me out and won't talk to me..."

When people come to me complaining of relational woes, this is what I hear most. Your frustration is valid, but the key takeaway here is to remember that people are different and understanding that others are different is the gateway to philia love. You can't expect another person to appreciate and understand love the same way that you do. That would be nice and simple, but life is anything but.

I've learned that many people love according to their capacity. We all have different levels of capacities to love. The more self-aware we become, the more our ability to love others deepens. If you understand your own love language, you can share with others ways that they can better show love to you by taking action yourself. Be the change you want. When you understand the primary love language of other people, you will discover how to love them right where they are.

HOW TO LOVE OTHERS: SEVEN KEY STRATEGIES

Being deeply loved by someone gives you strength, while loving someone deeply gives you courage.

— **Lao Tzu**

Here are seven practical strategies for learning how to love others. Remember, the first two most important strategies for loving others didn't make this list: loving God and loving yourself. We've already covered those in depth, but don't forget that Endless Love is a balancing act.

Whether you need to learn how to love your stubborn and intrusive mother-in-law, your neighbor who just won't stop mowing the lawn at 7:30 a.m. on a Sunday, or the friend who keeps canceling your coffee dates at the last minute, become a more loving person with these seven easy-to-implement strategies:

1. Love everyone's differences.

2. Humble yourself.

3. Be compassionate even if you lack understanding.

4. Show love to those who need it most and deserve it least.

5. Practice authenticity and vulnerability.

6. Just be there.

7. Let go and move on.

1) LOVE EVERYONE'S DIFFERENCES

Mastery of Endless Love is learning how to love everyone's differences. I will still love you, even if you look different from me, talk differently, dress differently, think differently, and yes, even if you *love* differently from me. I will love you right where you are. Your struggle is likely completely different from mine. What may be easy for one person may be the fight of another person's life. Love should not be conditional on commonality or similarity. We should love fiercely, love always, and without discourse.

The Bible has so much to say about loving differences. 1 Corinthians 12 says:

This makes for harmony among the members, so that all the members care for each other. If one part suffers, all the parts suffer with it, and if one part is honored, all the parts are glad. All of you together are Christ's body, and each of you is a part of it. [1Co 12:25-27 NLT]

Galatians 3:27-28 (another book in the Bible) adds:

For as many of you as were baptized into Christ have put on Christ. There is neither Jew nor Greek, there is neither slave nor free, there is no male and female, for you are all one in Christ Jesus. [Galatians 3:27-28 ESV]

People are different, and this is good. Imagine how boring life would be if we were all the same? If we all walked the same, talked the same, and liked all the same things, there would be no one to push us, disagree with us, or cause us to question why we like the things we do. The uniqueness of each individual is key to a well-versed, fully functional, and enjoyable society.

God created leaders to lead, listeners to listen, creatives to create, accountants to count, analysts to analyze, and dreamers to dream. God created every individual with a unique purpose and design that is likely far different from your own. If you don't get along with someone because they differ completely from you, try shifting the narrative you have of that person. Think about the amazing gifts they have that you don't. Consider all the ways you might even work with that person on a future project or goal. Opposites attract and fight harder than those who are similar, but multiple skill sets are key to accomplishing incredible things.

Learning how God gifted each of us is exciting. The church needs every single one of its members for the body to function at the highest level. No path and no purpose is the same, and understanding this is key to loving people of all types.

2) HUMBLE YOURSELF

As my career took off and life became more successful than I ever imagined it could, I always wanted to stay grounded. I intentionally put myself in situations where I needed to connect with individuals that weren't at the same level in their career. I never wanted to look down on others, no matter how big my title was. Humbling myself was important because I knew I was nothing without God. He doesn't look down upon me in shame; He lifts me up! My heart tells me to do the same for others, no matter their status.

When I became part of senior leadership and high-level executive staff, they expected me to behave a certain way and only engage with individuals that were acceptable to be seen with. I was told on several occasions: "Why are you speaking to that person? You have the potential to be a CEO... You need to watch who you're seen with!" Frequently during team lunches, I was told, "Stop talking with the waitress, she's the help. Know your place."

Would Jesus have ever not spoken to someone because they were the help? Of course not! It's ludicrous. Yet pride is one of many sins we need to be cognizant of, especially as we grow in self-awareness and make more out of our lives. If we aren't careful, we can quickly consider ourselves better than others. We need to eat with everybody, including sinners, just as Jesus did:

> *And as he reclined at a table in his house, many tax collectors and sinners were reclining with Jesus and his disciples, for there were many who followed him. [Mark 2:15 ESV]*

Tax collectors in Jesus' time were considered evil and the lowest of the low because they often cheated people out of their money. Be cognizant of who you spend the most time with and don't be afraid to humble yourself by talking with those less fortunate. Stand your ground even if your current tribe would prefer you speak only with them.

Ultimately, we are all at the same level and in need of the love of Christ. We are no better than the person passed out drunk in the street or the person talking loudly on their phone in line. Jesus loves that person the same amount as He loves us. There is no longer any separation because of God's love, and we would be wise to avoid creating barriers where there should only be love.

3) BE COMPASSIONATE EVEN IF YOU LACK UNDERSTANDING

Flatter me, and I may not believe you. Criticize me, and I may not like you. Ignore me, and I may not forgive you. Encourage me, and I will not forget you. Love me and I may be forced to love you.

— William Arthur Ward

God's love is eternal and far beyond our understanding. God's love is endless, and our capacity to understand is finite. The simple yet profound truth is that we don't have to understand each other to be able to love. We don't have to grasp why people act or think how they do to love them deeply. We can accept people exactly as they are, even if their lifestyle is completely different from our own. Even if we don't agree with the way they live their lives, we can show compassion and love them for who they are.

Compassion goes hand in hand with empathy. Empathy is the ability to put yourself in someone else's shoes and envision their hardships and struggles. Compassion is having a heart for that person and loving them as they are. Practice empathy in your heart and then show compassion out in the real world.

Smile at people who are homeless. Look them in the eye and show them warmth. Offer a kind word to the stressed-out guy next to you in line. Consider that the lady in the next lane who just cut you off might not have seen you and also just received terrible news from her doctor. Exercise your love muscle to be more like Jesus and love those people even when their actions throw us for a loop and make no sense.

4) SHOW LOVE TO THOSE WHO NEED IT MOST AND DESERVE IT LEAST

As you move forward with a deeper connection to God and with a cup that is more often full than not, you will see opportunities before you to give back and to love others. Be forewarned, this is where it gets tough! Now it's much harder to say no or turn a blind eye because you feel God's heart for that person as if they were your own child. Situations that might have brought on a long sigh or thoughts of judgment are suddenly seen through the eyes of God. Instead of a thief, you see someone in need. Instead of a careless driver, you see someone who's having a rough day. Instead of a boss testing the very limits of your patience, you see someone who also has a boss who's pressuring them too.

> "Come to me, **all you** who are weary and burdened, and I will give you rest. Take my yoke upon you and learn from me, for I am gentle and humble in heart, and you will find rest for your souls. [Mat 11:28-29 NIV emphasis mine]

Jesus is calling all to Him. Anyone can answer and follow Him. The good news of God is that we can come to Him, regardless. Extending the same grace to all who are hurting and in need is the goal, but of course, it's easier said than done.

When you see those less fortunate than you, show them love. Take a homeless person out for dinner. Buy groceries for the mother of three screaming kids standing in line in front of you. Give "the help," as my colleagues would call them, a big tip to show your appreciation. Do each with a smile and a warm heart. These acts of love may seem small, but you could change the person's day, or even their very lives, with your actions. Show love even when people don't deserve it. Show love even if people are mean, rude, or downright painful to be around. You never know if you might just break through the right barriers at the right time to reach a heart in need.

5) PRACTICE AUTHENTICITY AND VULNERABILITY

Authenticity is everything! You want to be proud of the person who's looking back at you in the mirror every morning. And you can only do that if you're being honest with yourself and being a person of genuine character. You have an opportunity every single day to write that story of your life.

— Aaron Rodgers, NFL Quarterback

Authenticity means being real with others. It means knowing yourself so well you can't help but be the real you, whomever you might be around. As mentioned previously, as you act like the real you, friends and family members might think you are being weird or not yourself, when in fact you are finally being the authentic you! This might turn people away at first, but eventually, you will attract the right people to you.

The very act of showing love is a deep act of vulnerability. We show authenticity when we open ourselves up to others. It's scary to do, and not something anyone particularly enjoys, but it's worth it as we grow into our ability to show love to others. Your authenticity and willingness to be vulnerable with people will be a measure of how much you love. Open up, share your heart, be the real you, and others will feel the love.

6) JUST BE THERE

In the chapter of Job in the Bible, we learn about a man who has everything taken away from him. He loses everything: his wealth, his family, and his livestock. God tested him in every way, and he's obviously hurting deeply. Luckily, he had three close friends who came to his side. Job's friends did what many would not, and they came to sit with him to mourn and to grieve with him, not saying a word, just being there:

> ***You have a right to be angry.*** *It's not negative or wrong. You don't have to condone someone's action or pretend you're okay with them to be a good or spiritual person. Just know that you have the power to move beyond your pain when you're ready. You have the power to find lessons in your heartache, gains in your losses, and reasons to forgive. It might take time, and it might not be easy, but it is possible to heal and move on.*
>
> **— Lori Deschene-**

Job lost everything. He was sick and hurting. All he needed was someone to be there with him through the pain. There was nothing any one person could do to ease his predicament. It was beyond the ability of any human to fix. The best anyone could do was to sit next to him and encourage.

We all need each other. Once you get better at self-love, don't get stuck in the rut of defaulting to alone time. Research has proven that loneliness is on the rise, and this lack of human connection can be more harmful to your health than obesity, smoking, and even high blood pressure.[13] The good news is that we can combat loneliness with the simple act of just being there for others.

Everyone has hidden issues we may never discover. It's normal to go through stuff. The global pandemic that started in 2020 affected most of the world's seven billion people. No one escaped unscathed. It's important to remember that the best thing we can do is just to be there for people, just like Job's friends were there for him. Be a shoulder to cry on or an ear to listen. Let them know: "Hey, I got your back. I'm here even if I don't know what you're going through. I'm here for you."

We won't always understand what people are going through. To us, it might be trivial or something we've dealt with 100 times already, but to that person, it's everything. All it takes is being intentional about showing up. Just be there for other people:

---

[13] House, James S., et al. "Social Relationships and Health." Science, vol. 241, no. 4865, 1988, pp. 540–45. Crossref, doi:10.1126/science.3399889.

- Call and ask your friend how they are doing and listen actively to their answer. Show them support by staying on the phone as long as they need.

- Bring a hot meal to a friend who's hurting because they just lost a loved one.

- Write a letter to a family member telling them what you appreciate about them and mail it in a fancy envelope.

- Practice empathy and put yourself in their shoes. As you listen, engage with them and picture their situation as if you were going through it.

- Don't get nervous or feel you need to do more than just show up. So often, we second guess our actions and think that we didn't do or say enough, when we just need to take a deep breath and remember that our presence likely meant a lot to the other person. Time is a valuable commodity that we can give freely to those in need.

7) LET GO AND MOVE ON

I've had relationships where I stayed too long, and it became difficult to walk away because of the long-term commitment. I felt more obligated to the other person's feelings and lifestyle than to my own. I was giving 80% and the other person was responding with 20%. I started recognizing a pattern in my relationships. I didn't understand why I wasn't taking care of myself and why

I felt obligated to make sure my actions satisfied the other person. I didn't realize I had a root of rejection, and a fear of letting other people down, even if it was costing me everything.

It wasn't until I sat down and analyzed each relationship (both past and present) that I discovered how much I was giving and, ultimately, how much I was losing. I had to take accountability for each interaction, good or bad. I discovered during my analysis that I endured destructive behavior and toxic people because of my fear of rejection and being alone. When I thought about the details of some of the toxic situations I was in, I became bitter. I internalized my emotions and my desires because I thought the other person would have empathy for me and change their behavior. It's common to think that our newfound awareness should also be obvious to others, but they remain as blind now as we used to be. They became accustomed to being served, and I became accustomed to submitting and serving.

The consistent torture and pain of an unfulfilled life is a reminder that your situation must change. Sometimes, no matter how much we give and how badly we want things to change, there is nothing we can do to help another person see the light. The best way forward is to let go. This is coming from someone who learned this lesson the hard way (as is often the case), but I would love to help pull you forward out of your current situation, so that both you and the other person will experience more love. Because sometimes, you see, the most loving thing you can do is let go.

We hold on to things and people that keep us bound and without room to breathe. We adapt to lifestyles and mindsets that were never intended for us. We all come here on our own separate paths. Sometimes these separate paths connect and paint a beautiful tapestry that lasts for a lifetime. Other times, these paths come together only for a short period. Still, other times, the paths of certain individuals clash with no hope of restoration. Relationships are a major factor to your success or failure in life. Knowing when to let go in life can be one of the toughest challenges you will face. The key is to take this difficult step and move on.

You don't have to master these seven strategies for loving others all at once. Please, don't try! Instead, take it one day at a time and improve slowly. Pick one or two that you can get started on today and make progress as you navigate the complexities of relationships.

WHEN LOVE IS DIFFICULT

"Jesus talked to His friends a lot about how we should identify ourselves. He said it wouldn't be what we said we believed or all the good we hoped to do someday. Nope, He said we would identify ourselves simply by how we loved people. It's tempting to think there is more to it, but there's not. Love isn't something we fall into; love is someone we become."

— Bob Goff, Everybody, Always[14]

---

[14] Goff, Bob. Everybody Always: Becoming Love in a World Full of Setbacks and Difficult People. 1st ed., Nelson Books, 2018.

The above quote from bestselling author and speaker Bob Goff is good to remember, because it can be extremely difficult to love some people. But as he says, "love is someone we become." This becoming will stretch us to the limits of our capabilities and patience! But ultimately, we need to go through the struggle to learn how to love. You can't start a fire without friction. Love often comes via pain and hardship.

Understanding the five love languages is a great first step, but not everyone is easy to love and willing to accept the love you're giving to them. Learning and practicing the seven ways to love others is great but loving certain people will always prove more difficult than it should. People with unresolved issues are usually the hardest people to love, and it might become difficult to put our emotions in check so that we can still love them. Difficult people make their personal issues everybody else's problem, but often won't even listen to advice. They're the people stuck in their fixed mindset and won't make any attempt to understand their own love language, yet alone understand yours!

I have met people who, at first glance, you think are super successful. Their lives were jacked up and they had a lot of problems. I used to put these individuals on a pedestal because I thought the package, they were wrapped in was worthy of royalty. But then when I opened the package and looked inside, it wasn't as royal or as attractive as I thought it was. It was a total mess. I saw them for who they really were. I quickly realized their external appearance looked nothing like the internal.

I evaluated relationships in my life and realized some friendships became a revolving door (coming and going) back into my life, asking for my advice, resenting me for giving my honest opinion, and then leaving yet again. Eventually, I learned to shut the door before things went too far and to keep healthy boundaries up to block people from taking up all my time.

I've learned no matter how educated, attractive, physically fit, or intellectual you are, we all have an area that needs work, and not everyone will like you. Hurting people hurt others. People who are in pain will bring you into their pain, and you must be ready and prepared to put your armor on.

I used to think I needed to help change those around me, even if they were prideful and not willing to change. I didn't understand why they didn't see the world as I saw it. I've encountered older people that complain about everything and every word they spoke had a bitter sound to it. I've found that relatives can be the most challenging to love because we know each other's faults, so we hold those things against each other. Random strangers can sometimes be the rudest people but are often the most kind.

The downfall of going beyond what you're capable of and rising up is that you see just how stuck other people are. You can't help but feel waves of judgment because you KNOW they can do more. It hurts you deeply because you can see a path forward for them that would remove many of their difficulties, but they won't listen, even if you tell them! Many people are stuck, and don't want to get unstuck. As you make progress and get out of whatever pit you are in, you will face the same reality.

To be in the presence of these types of people used to irritate me. I took energy and time (that I can never get back) to speak directly into the lives of women on the same path I used to be on. It did more harm than good. They didn't know that, as a woman, they should desire some form of independence and should strive for more in their lives. I didn't get why they depended on the system to care for them and why they waited for someone else to fix their problems. Several times I caused disagreements with relatives because I didn't agree with their lifestyle. But I had to examine why I felt like it was my business to correct them. I had the mentality that because they *could* be better, it meant they *needed* to make progress right *now* on *my* timeline for them.

No matter how much I cared or shared my opinion, it didn't change their mindset. It only made them angry because they misunderstood. My intentions were good, but my execution was poor. They felt judged, and I made them feel like I was better than them. But that wasn't my intention. I certainly didn't feel as if I was better than them. I sincerely cared for them, and I wanted more for them. I put myself in their shoes and remembered when I was struggling to find my way. I was depending on the system and had the desire to do more and be more, but I realized just how much we all are in need of love.

In my personal story of abuse, I was the victim, and I suffered at the hands of those tasked with protecting me. There is no excuse for their behavior, but the reality is those individuals were broken too. They needed fixing just as I have needed fixing. It doesn't mean what they did is okay (far from it!), but it's important to remember that everyone is on a different path. Not everyone is ready to own their truth about life, but you still have the agency to become better.

Love is difficult. Love is complicated. Love is everything, and yet it feels so far away for certain people. When things get really difficult, take a step back. When people don't show you the same level of love back, think about your motivation for staying in your current situation. Love fiercely and with more vigor if you need to. Let go if that's the best option. When love gets difficult, make a choice for how you want to move forward and own your decision.

LIVING IN COMMUNITY

Building a thriving community is the end goal of loving others. When you live in an engaging community, you truly feel the love. A high-functioning and loving community supports, encourages, and checks in with each of its members. The magic is that you can build this community anywhere. It's a challenging task, and tough to get right, but you can form it by taking action with God's help.

Community doesn't solely exist at church, at town hall budget meetings, or within your family. You can build community at work, with the people you exercise with, or the people you see on the street. There is no limit to pushing the boundaries on what might become a community. In fact, community goes far beyond being related by blood, and is far more powerful. Some of the most loving and closest communal connections I have had have been outside the bonds of family.

Building community starts with showing up and being present in people's lives. Attend or organize weekend meetup groups with your coworkers, schedule a time to serve at a local homeless shelter with friends, join a local sports group and get to know the people you're playing with by having a drink after the competition. No matter what you do, think of ways you can create or enhance the current community you're in.

Merriam-Webster defines community as:

"A unified body of individuals: such as a group of people with a common characteristic or interest living together within a larger society."[15]

The first part, "a unified body of individuals," strikes a major chord in the song that is Endless Love. Community unifies us in our pursuit of overcoming adversity. We have all faced some pretty crazy stuff like the pandemic of 2020-21 that just won't seem to end. Being there for each other and serving as an anchor point for someone going through a tough time is the true magic of living and breathing in community.

---

[15] "Community." The Merriam-Webster.Com Dictionary, www.merriam-webster.com/dictionary/community. Accessed 21 Dec. 2021.

If we can more easily trust others, bring family into community alongside us, and build community wherever we go, we will be one step closer to living out love for others. If we learn to put others first, we would be ever closer to existing as a calm and peaceful society. This is the ideal, but nowhere near impossible. Strong community and togetherness is how we will do it. I hope you join me.

PRACTICING ENDLESS LOVE

- **Pray:** *Lord, help me love others and rely on you for understanding. Give me the patience I need to deal with troublesome people that will enter my life. Help me humble myself and remember the importance of each encounter I have. I know I don't have to be perfect, but that you expect the best that I can give. Help me give my best at each moment of every day. Help me love endlessly. Help me to be better. Help me overcome anything holding me back from being the most loving person I can be. I need you now and forever in all that I do. Go ahead of me and prepare the way. Thank you, Lord! Amen!*

- **Read:** Bob Goff writes with love in mind. Two of his books, *Love Does*, and *Everybody Always*, are great reads to learn how to live in love. His desire is to be more like Jesus in all that he does, and the stories he tells illustrates how he works toward this goal every day. Add his books to your reading list.

- **Act:** Pick one strategy for becoming a more loving person and do it this week. Take a step of faith to become love. Trust that God will guide you and be with you every step of the way. You are never alone. God is always with you. Keep on growing stronger in love.

CHAPTER FOUR
MAKING TREASURE OUT OF TRASH

Be alert and of sober mind. Your enemy the devil prowls around like a roaring lion looking for someone to devour. 1 Peter 5:8

Growing up, I believed in monsters under the bed. Why? Because in my crazy life, snakes appear anywhere they like...

Early one evening when I was just a kid, not long after the incident where my mother's husband passed away, my mother was sweeping the floor in her bedroom. Suddenly, I heard a shriek, and she called after me. I was in the living room watching TV as she called for me. I walked into her bedroom and noticed her with her back up against the wall. "Do you see that!?" she hastily said to me as she pointed underneath the bed.

I looked down and I will never forget what I saw. The memory of it will be etched on my brain forever. A huge black snake slithered out from under her bed. We lived on the top floor of an apartment building in SouthEast Washington, D.C. There was no reason for a snake to be up that high or anywhere near us. We had never seen one before, so it was quite a shock.

After confirming to my mother that I could, in fact, see the snake and that she wasn't crazy, I ran out of the room. From that day on, I was paranoid. I always looked under my sheets and under my bed before getting in bed. I would look for monsters under the bed and behind doors. I started asking other kids in my neighborhood, "have you ever seen a snake in your house?" Everyone I asked said "no." I couldn't shake the image of that snake slithering towards us from under the bed, and to be honest, I don't think I ever truly will.

Seeing that snake felt like a bad omen and a sign for things to come. Things got worse for us each day. My mother was having a hard time coping with the loss of her husband and the aftermath of suddenly having to raise her kids alone with minimal help. It was a rough time for me and for my family, but there is always a silver lining, always something to be thankful for.

Eventually, we left the apartment and moved in with family in the suburbs. This was a difficult transition for us and for our relatives. I had to leave the school I liked, which also meant leaving after-school programs and teachers that had kept me grounded. I was resilient and adjusted quickly, but it still felt unfair to me at the time.

There was compromise on both sides, and I am grateful now for an extended family who gave us a hand when we needed it most. My cousin gave up his privacy for all of us to share his room. The three of us slept in his bed and he slept on the couch. Mornings were rough since we shared one bathroom amongst five kids (three girls and two boys).

At first, we argued almost every day about everything. As the weeks passed, we settled into the new environment and fell into a new "normal." I met kids my age nearby and became close friends with a young girl across the street. This helped pass the time and turned my focus away from the drama of my life. My new friend and I started doing everything together. We had so many sessions where we would get together and just laugh and find silly things to do. It was truly a blessing to meet her. I had found my treasure in the trash.

I look back on this time with mixed memories. Sharing a bed with your two siblings and sharing a bathroom with five people might be okay for a weekend get together, but as a living arrangement, it sucked. I hated it. But I also wouldn't have met my friend, who gave me hope and joy when I needed it most. There is always something good if you look hard enough, even if all seems lost, unfair, or insurmountable.

THE BELLY OF THE BEAST

Darkness cannot drive out darkness: only light can do that. Hate cannot drive out hate: only love can do that.

— Martin Luther King Jr.

What is something good in your life?

Think about your answer for a second. Don't skip this question with an "everything sucks" or the even worse response "everything is okay." Everything doesn't suck, and everything is definitely not okay. You might be at a point when all the walls around you are threatening to box you in. You might feel that there isn't any hope. You might feel like Endless Love isn't possible for you because you just have too much going on. You might have fallen into apathy, and you just don't care anymore. Let this question be the life raft that pulls you safely onto shore.

When everything around you looks and sounds like hell, reaching for heaven is difficult. Feeling God's presence might be even harder. Life circumstances will test your resolve and willingness to grow. If you're willing to endure the pain and eventually triumph, you will be stronger for it. The resilience you build over time will never leave you, and you will surprise yourself at your newfound strength.

Your environment and the family you are born into plays a significant role in your outcome. Some people will fight harder than others to overcome their environment and circumstances. The most frustrating part is that you can't choose it! You're stuck dealing with whatever environment and circumstance you find yourself in. There's no genie in a bottle who will come and whisk you away on a magic carpet. When you're in the belly of the beast, it's up to you to get out.

Avoid comparing your journey to anyone else's. This is the fastest way to stay stuck. What may be easy for one person may be the fight of another person's life. What might be difficult for you is a piece of cake for someone else. If you are lacking resources, support, and opportunities, the desired change might take longer than expected. However long you take to overcome will be however long you take to overcome. There is no right or wrong as long as you're moving ahead.

Each of us was born with different circumstances and personal challenges. Some of us start with humble beginnings and lack the support and nourishment from loving parents or extended family members. Some of us might have physical or mental problems and very few resources available to us from the start. Others start their lives with perfect genes, a supportive and loving family, and tons of money. Not all who start well end up successful, and not all who start from behind end up in shambles.

Your environment shapes your mind and your character. If a child faces adverse circumstances, it usually results in poor mental and emotional development which they need to overcome. If the foundation is not strong in the development years, it will be even more challenging for this child later on. If you come from a dysfunctional environment, you will probably face doubt, unbelief, and insecurity. We can only live within this dysfunction for so long until it turns toxic and invades our very minds and changes the way we think about life and love. It's so toxic it becomes our new normal, and we don't see the toxic fumes all around us!

No matter your circumstance, it's up to you to pave your way forward. No one is coming to save you or hold your hand through the long process of becoming more loving. I waited for my superhero to come and rescue me, but they never never came. That auntie or uncle never rose as a mentor to take care of me and lead me on. My dad silently removed himself, and my mother was emotionally unavailable. No one was reaching out their hand to pull me up, so I pulled myself up.

The pain and hardship drove me upwards. It pushed me to make a way for myself and to reject the vices surrounding me. It felt good to push myself to the next level and to want more from my life. It took longer than I would have liked, but once I made up my mind, there was no going back.

I was ready for the challenge. Physical fitness became a great outlet for me and helped me sort out a lot of my issues. Working towards my next physical fitness goal took the pain away. I didn't think about what was lacking in my life or how painful the exercise was. I just did it. Get over your desire to blame others and

God. Become driven by the pain of knowing what will happen if you stop.

Making treasure out of trash and overcoming the belly of the beast starts with building an awareness of your need to give and receive love. It starts with a positive outlook and a fervent dedication to being your own hero. You can make gold out of dirt if you believe in a God who loves you and wants you to take the next step. Don't wait for someone else to do it for you. Dig in and get to work.

WATCH OUT FOR THESE SEVEN ROADBLOCKS TO LIVING IN LOVE

As you grow in love by connecting deeper with God, yourself, and others, challenging life circumstances will come at you. Just like the black snake that had no business being underneath my mom's bed, life has the nasty habit of throwing a curveball at you the moment you decide to make a change. I want you to be ready for whatever life throws at you and to move beyond so you can practice Endless Love.

The following are seven roadblocks you will encounter at some point or another in your journey toward Endless Love. These roadblocks are hard to avoid life events. I want to be clear that each one of these likely deserves their own book, but as awareness is key, I wanted to do my part to prepare you for what's ahead. Endless Love can truly conquer all if we accept and embrace it fully. This list is not exhaustive, but it's filled with issues I've faced and overcome on my journey:

1. Cyber Illusion.

2. The question "why?"

3. Health problems.

4. Grief and loss.

5. The valley.

6. Family.

7. Hopelessness.

1) CYBER ILLUSION

Do not be conformed to this world, but be transformed by the renewal of your mind, that by testing you may discern what is the will of God, what is good and acceptable and perfect. [Rom 12:2 ESV]

Many of us are lost and lack understanding in a world that is quickly evolving into what I call "Cyber Illusion." The culture we live in today is radically different from the one our parents and grandparents grew up in. Life is full of reality TV shows that are not reality. Never ending social media feeds keep you up to date on the latest gossip and the best-dressed celebrities. Its goal is to keep you sedated and focused on foolish things. The important things in life go unattended while you scroll for an average of two hours every day.[16]

A fascinating study in 2016,[17] conducted by researchers at Penn State University, suggested that when participants viewed other people's selfies, it lowered their own self-esteem. People compare their current selves to photos of others looking their happiest and at their best. Research from the University of Strathclyde, Ohio University, and University of Iowa also found that women compare themselves negatively to selfies of other women.[18] This is just a taste of Cyber Illusion and it's dangerous effects. Social media has the power to change your view on reality if you allow it.

Social media plays a huge part in our lives. It's glued us to our devices and almost everyone owns a social media account: Instagram, Facebook, Twitter, TikTok, etc. Men and women create false illusions on social media showing the average person to be something they are not. Many people use these images to compare themselves to an ideal that is impossible to live up to.

When you're not able to keep up or compete with the images, it can be dangerous. Some people are not mentally strong

---

[16] Mander, Jason, and Jason Mander. "Daily Time Spent on Social Networks Rises to Over 2 Hours." GWI, 27 Nov. 2019, blog.gwi.com/chart-of-the-day/daily-time-spent-on-social-networks.

[17] Wang, Ruoxu, et al. "Let Me Take a Selfie: Exploring the Psychological Effects of Posting and Viewing Selfies and Groupies on Social Media." Telematics and Informatics, vol. 34, no. 4, 2017, pp. 274–83. Crossref, doi:10.1016/j.tele.2016.07.004.

[18] Briggs, By Helen. "'Selfie' Body Image Warning Issued." BBC News, 10 Apr. 2014, www.bbc.co.uk/news/health-26952394.

enough to separate these images (on social media or TV) from reality. Many people go to extreme measures like plastic surgery and body enhancements to make themselves more perfect. This quest for perfection of body isn't necessary. You are perfect, just as you are, but we wash away this fundamental truth in a sea of phoniness.

We've developed into a world of fiction and make believe. A society that takes pleasure in reality-based shows creates chaos and turmoil because we inevitably compare ourselves to others and wish we could be more like our "heroes." Society views women as symbols of sex, property, and displays our gender as rigid, angry, self-centered, and selfish. With our current culture, society leaves little room for mistakes or errors. They won't let you forget when you have messed up. Forgiveness is a foreign concept, and it's difficult to redeem yourself when you've done something "unforgivable."

Cyber Illusion presents a tricky problem, because we have to be constantly on our guard as we use technology. We need not be ignorant of the world and what's going on in it, but we have to guard our hearts relentlessly, lest the enemy find a foothold. The internet is one of humanity's greatest inventions, but it has wrought chaos as well as good fortune.

Awareness, as always, is the first step. Become more aware of the shows you watch, the podcasts you listen to, and even the books you read. Be cognizant of who you follow on social media and be honest with your thoughts as you scroll. Limit time spent on your phone to a bare minimum. Don't let Instagram or Tik-Tok be your wake up call every day. Do more activities with your hands like writing letters, playing outside, or going for a long walk with someone special. Slow down by reducing the constant pressure of social media to perform and to always be living your best life.

2) THE QUESTION "WHY?"

The trials of life will bring you down on your knees asking God:

"Why! Why!? Why did this happen to me? Why aren't you answering my prayers? Why do I have to go through this? What do I have to learn? Why aren't you protecting me? Why have you gone away?"

I've been there with tears in my eyes, frequently weeping for God to relieve my pain. I imagine you've had similar times in your life? Maybe you haven't yet gone to God with the question why, but it's no doubt crossed your mind. We all wonder why we have to suffer through our various trials. We all wish we didn't have to deal.

Getting down on your knees is the first step. When life deals you a wicked blow, your go-to first step is kneeling in prayer. Putting yourself in a posture of prayer and surrender opens up your heart and mind to what God wants to say to you. Listen to Him. He likely won't answer with absolute clarity and tell you exactly why you are going through what you are going through, but He will be right there with you.

Unfortunately, we won't know until we get to heaven why a lot of things happened to us. God certainly has a plan, but it is beyond our ability to understand. This level of trust makes following God difficult, but it's faith that we must grow. God wants us to trust Him regardless of what happens to us, just like Job did in our story earlier in the book.

Ask God why. He may answer, he may not. Yell, scream, weep, cast all your cares upon Him. He is God and He can take everything you can throw at Him. Listen with an intent to hear and a heart to follow no matter what. You may never know why things happen the way they do, but always ask. Start a communication with God straight from the heart.

3) HEALTH PROBLEMS

Whether it's mental or physical, most of us will face health problems at various times in our lives. Yes, you might have that great grandfather who never went to the doctor and lived until he was 104, but this is uncommon. The health problem I faced is one I wouldn't wish on my worst enemy, and it came on without warning.

I was thirty-seven and thriving in my career. I was eager to wake up and go to work each morning. The hunt for success fueled my footsteps. No matter what was going on in my personal life, I could go to work and leave my worries behind. Work motivated me and invigorated me. I stayed on the move with no time to think about what was worrying me or what wasn't going right in my life.

I was healthy, strong, and physically fit. I felt like I could take on the world. If a problem presented itself on the job, I had the solution. If I didn't have an immediate solution, I did the research to find a fix. My daily mission was to focus on the current project and get the job done. I had the work ethic and the self-motivation to accomplish any task set before me and to do it well.

But for some reason, I suddenly felt different from before. I have overcome so much in my life that I thought I knew what pain felt like. I was wrong. I was experiencing pain throughout my entire body, the likes of which I've never had before. It was a strange pain that was difficult to explain or understand. Even thinking back, it's hard to put into words just how much pain I was in. In the beginning, I ignored the signs because I thought I was a healthy eater, so naturally I should be fine, right? I didn't eat meat or dairy and I ate plenty of fruits and vegetables. I thought it would pass on its own, no problem. Then my skin started changing. I noticed dryness around my eyes and blotchiness in my face. No matter how much moisturizer or products I used, my skin did not look healthy.

The pain and discomfort showed up more often. I slept more frequently, and I needed naps throughout the day. I remember going to work one day exhausted after getting a full night's sleep. I was having problems staying awake during the day to perform normal activities. Of course, I thought, "I'm stressed, I need more rest, and need to take more time to prepare my meals at home." But it was obvious something was wrong.

I tried incorporating even more fruits and vegetables into my diet, went to bed earlier, and even pulled back from social events. I tried a myriad of other things meant to heal my body. My symptoms were not only not getting better, they were getting worse. I started having severe pain in my joints, swelling around my ankles, heart palpitations, and throbbing, sharp pain on one side of the body.

I didn't talk about what I was feeling or experiencing to anyone. Honestly, I didn't think anyone would listen to me or believe me. Besides, I am the one everyone else comes to when they're not feeling well or need a word of wisdom. Who could help me like I was helping everyone else?

I knew at this point I had to see my doctor, so I booked an appointment. She ordered several tests, which all returned with a negative result. It only took a couple of appointments to know she was giving up and was thinking I was crazy. Which, unfortunately, is all too common. Our relationship slowly diminished. Her final words to me during our last appointment were, "Ms. Moore, we can't find anything wrong with you, you must be suffering from stress." I looked at the doctor and responded, "Yes I have plenty of stress in my life, but something else is wrong." I wanted to add a "duh" but I didn't out of respect.

I wasn't ignorant of the dangers of stress and I knew that my issue went beyond being stress induced. That evening I went home disappointed, annoyed, and more than a little hopeless. I didn't blame the doctor; she could only give advice based on her experience and education. It was up to me to find the answer to my problem, but I knew I wasn't alone. I did what I knew best. I got on my knees and asked God what to do and how to move forward. God once again proved to be my rock and my comfort.

Remember fasting, one of the seven disciplines for growing closer to God from chapter one? I started fasting for an answer to what was going on with my body. I spent time with God, not eating, and listening to what He had to say. It will never cease to amaze me that God is for us in each area of our lives. We merely need to listen. I heard God say get another doctor and ask for a second opinion, even though the first experience was so unhelpful.

I contacted my healthcare provider and asked to be assigned to another physician. I made my first appointment and gave the doctor a rundown of my symptoms, giving as much detail as possible. The doctor looked at me and stated, "I am going to give you a test, but I don't want to tell you the name of the test because I don't want to scare you. We usually have to perform this test in order to identify this as the problem, so let's see what results we get." It sounded ominous, but I thought, what the heck? Ignorance isn't bliss, and I was ready for anything as long as it wasn't another dark and winding path leading nowhere.

We performed the test that day and she informed me she would contact me with the results that evening. Later that evening, the doctor called me, and she started by saying, "I have good news and I have bad news. Which do you want first?"

I responded, "Give it to me straight. I need a name for this so I can fight it."

She said, "You tested positive for lupus, but your numbers are low so we can control it with diet and exercise."

I informed her I don't plan to merely control the disease because I was not keeping it. Although the diagnosis was a positive reading, I was relieved. Even though 10-15% of people with lupus die from it,[19] I was determined not to be a statistic. Now that I knew what I was dealing with, the fight was on. At the time, I knew little about lupus. However, I knew it wasn't a friendly disease and you can die a slow, painful death if you don't manage it properly.

I discovered a history of the disease in my mom's family and learned that my grandmother and aunt died from it. I have an aunt living with the disease and unfortunately, my mother was diagnosed with the disease in 2019. Initially, I saw my life flash before my eyes; I saw myself in a casket. My desire to live a healthy and fulfilling life fueled me with determination. I would defeat lupus and ensure it wouldn't become my legacy. I was

---

[19] Wallace, D.J., & Hahn, B.H. (2013). Dubois' lupus erythematosus and related syndromes. (8th ed.) Philadelphia, PA: Elsevier Saunders.

ready to fight back and feel better. I was prepared for the challenge, even though I knew it wouldn't be easy. I started my journey by going to God for wisdom. My day started with prayer each morning and fasting became a lifestyle for me.

Still, my situation confused and angered me. This is natural, and if you encounter your own major health problems, you have every right to feel this way, too. How could I be this young and health conscious and still experience such a painful disease? I was consistent with my healthy lifestyle and physical fitness. At least, I thought I was making healthy choices. But no matter how hard we try or how "good" we do, it might not be enough. Our Earthly bodies are finite and won't last. We can fight to preserve, and healthy eating and exercise is important, but we have to realize we are fighting a losing battle against time. One day we will die. We can only prolong the inevitable.

The danger of this roadblock is that we become so focused on getting healthy and feeling better that we revert to 100% self-love. Yes, of course we might need to take a step back to heal, but so often when we are sick and hurting we lose all touch with the world and even with God. We need to learn to accept medical issues for what they are, expect that we will run into them, and not let them pull us into a downward spiral where they become the only thing we focus on. Endless Love cannot exist if we spend every second of our day worrying about or trying to fix our disease.

If you're struggling with a medical issue or a mental problem, seek help. Don't go it alone and don't Google your symptoms. This is the last thing you should do! Instead, eat healthy foods. Exercise. Do what needs to be done to feel better, but don't make it your everything. This is much easier said than done, but ask yourself how much time you spend worrying about symptoms X Y or Z and be real. Shift your focus to a mindset of feeling better and stop spending more time than is necessary dealing with your issues.

4) GRIEF AND LOSS

"It hurts to live after someone has died. It just does. It can hurt to walk down a hallway or open the fridge. It hurts to put on a pair of socks, to brush your teeth. Food tastes like nothing. Colors go flat. Music hurts, and so do memories. You look at something you'd otherwise find beautiful—a purple sky at sunset or a playground full of kids—and it only somehow deepens the loss. Grief is so lonely this way."

— Michelle Obama, Becoming[20]

Whether it's the loss of a loved one, a close mentor, or a friend we love, grief and loss will strike all of us in our lives. It's an inevitable, albeit horrible, truth of life. We cannot avoid it. We can prepare our hearts by allowing the eternal love of God to

---

[20] Obama, Michelle. Becoming. 1st Edition, Crown, 2018.

fill us up, but we cannot prepare fully for the pain of tragic loss and the prevailing winds of grief which follow. The best way to prepare is to live in love.

Be there for others as they go through trials. If they are going through grief and loss, you can partly prepare yourself for going through something like it in the future, but also ensure you have others who will be there for you when you are going through something. Those who you help will not always come through for you at your time of need, but some will. Build a community of fellow believers, deep friends, and all-around good people.

As grief and loss strike you and the people around you, don't be afraid to dive in. Of course, be cognizant of your own cup and be sure it's not nearing empty, but lean into hardship to build resilience. Talk with friends who've gone through really tough things. As you comfort them, listen intently to any strategies that are working for them. It's not all about you, so build your strength for any tough times ahead by giving back and being there for other people during their time of grief.

In her book, *On Death and Dying*, Elisabeth Kübler-Ross brought to light the five stages of coping with dying (DABDA).[21] These stages are:

- **Denial:** Refusing to believe that what's happening is actually happening. "This can't be happening."

---

[21] Kubler-Ross, Elisabeth. On Death And Dying. 1st ed., Scribner, 2014.

- **Anger:** Being in a heightened sense of frustration about the current circumstances. "I'm deeply upset that this is happening to me."

- **Bargaining:** Pleading with God to remove the grief in exchange for something else. "God, if you bring my mother back, I promise never to sin again."

- **Depression:** Being deeply upset about the loss. "This suck and there's nothing I can do about it."

- **Acceptance:** Finally accepting the truth about what has happened. "I'm not okay with what happened, but I accept it and I will do my best to move on."

There's no need to recite these verbatim to a hurting friend. And please, for the love of all that is holy, do NOT tell your friend which stage of grief they are in. It's more than enough to just be aware so you can be there for them and know what they need and know too what you might face in the future.

5) THE VALLEY

In the valley, I was the go-to person for all the world's problems. I could listen and hear what was being said and what needed to be said. I would comfort them, cheer them on, and make it a priority to care for them. I clarified that God is for them, and I was there for them, too.

While in the valley, I heard from struggling people daily. I held daily counseling sessions and advised them without the monetary reward or the recognition. It was my mission to uplift, comfort, and motivate the lowly, the deprived, and the rejected. They could always count on me to be there for them. It didn't matter what was happening in my life or how much I was lacking and suffering. I was there for them in the valley when they needed me. But once they were better, I'd be alone in the valley until the next inevitable visitor. The valley kept me company, but slowly became my prison.

The hurting would come and go at different times in my life. When they received their redemption, they would quickly leave the valley. My services were no longer required. No phone call, no wellness checks, just poof! Gone, just like that. Looking back, I have a bitter taste in my mouth because yes; I was helping people, but they always left me feeling used and abused, as if all they wanted was help and cared nothing about me.

I noticed a pattern. People would come into my life and recognize the gift that was in me. They did not genuinely want me; they wanted what I offered. They wanted help for themselves and that's it. I gave of myself freely, putting myself last and others first. I even rejected my children and other areas of my life to help others. I thought the noble thing to do when a friend is in pain was to drop everything to help them.

It took me years to realize the reason I could help others in the valley was because I mastered the valley. I lived on valley street and valley state. It was my home for years. I didn't understand why I continued in the same cycles in my life for years with no change, but I was good at being stuck.

No matter how many times I prayed, fasted, and went to church, it did not change what was going on inside of me. The love and compassion I projected to others was the love and compassion I lacked in my personal life.

I didn't realize how damaged I was. I used the valley as a mask to hide my pain. I wore that mask for years and stayed put.

To get out of the valley and stay out, I knew I had to be my own hero. I had to take charge of my life and drive the direction. It took years to soar high enough above the valley to even understand that I was in it! I had finally gained understanding and awareness of the valley.

Once I realized no one was coming to rescue me, I knew it was time for *me* to rescue *me*. I didn't know how I was going to do it. I just knew it was time. It took far too long to get to this point.

Years of pain and misery brought me to my wit's end.

You might be in the valley right now. Do you know? Here are a few telltale signs you are deep in the valley and that it might be time for you to come up for a breath of fresh air:

- You seek other forms of relief from the pain of life, such as sex, alcohol, too much TV, or another addiction.

- You find it hard to love yourself and give yourself the attention you deserve.

- God feels distant and your prayers feel unanswered.

- Your cup has been empty for years, and you don't know how to fill it up. All you know is helping others.

- You lack the motivation or drive to do anything to improve your situation.

When I was finally alone in the valley after I helped everyone else escape, I realized the valley was in me. I was creating the prison I was living in. No matter how much I would mask my pain, it would appear in different areas of my life.

Finally, I fought to appreciate my time in the valley but also made moves to escape its clutches. It's my hope that my words here will pull you out of the valley much quicker.

What moves do you need to make to grow in self-awareness? It's okay to be where you are right now, but don't stay there. Take positive action to get yourself out of the valley and to stay out. You don't need to race out as fast as you can. Take your time to change. Your ultimate ability to help people will be much stronger once you are out of the valley and well beyond the reach of this painful roadblock.

6) FAMILY

It may surprise you to see that I included family as a major roadblock. But think about it, is anyone devoid of family issues? Of course, our families can be the best thing about our lives, but sometimes it takes an incredible amount of effort to get to a place of peace and harmony instead of hot mess and discord. Sometimes (not always, but sometimes) it's not worth the struggle to get things right. It might be a much better choice to move on rather than attempt healing. Relationships deep in love and trust often get there through fire, but if the fire burns you from head to toe, is it worth it?

I have an extended view of family, because I consider some of my best friends to be my family. But with this expanded definition, so too also comes the same family challenges. For years, I endured abuse from family and those who called themselves "friends." I learned that just because you are related through blood doesn't mean you are family. Families comprise people that love and support one another. It doesn't matter your color, creed, gender or ethnicity; if we love and support each other, we are family. If things become toxic, painful, or bring us down far more often than they lift us up, it might be time to move on and cut ties. This action might be the hardest thing you've ever done, but it might just be the most beneficial to your long-term health and wellbeing and to your ability to love fiercely.

As I learned to let go, it was painful to disconnect myself emotionally from individuals I grew up with and had so many intimate experiences with. Too often, we hold on to relationships and traditions by default because it's been passed down to us.

My abusers were those close to me that knew me intimately. They were individuals I looked up to and interacted with every day.

I suffered in silence for years and said nothing and did nothing. I stayed in the valley with little help and no support. My mind would race from one toxic event to another.

I kept myself busy to mask the pain.

Relationship commitments are important, and you shouldn't ignore responsibilities, but open your heart to new options if you need them. People around you are not "family" if they treat you poorly, abuse you, or are never around when you're the one needing help. Family members who abuse you, put you down, or demand more from you than you can give are not family. Let my words here be the permission you never really needed to cut ties and move on if it's becoming too much to bear. Maybe, one day, the relationship might heal and be better than ever. Space and time work wonders to repair broken relationships, so never lose hope, even if you need to separate for a time.

Family isn't meant to be experienced as I have experienced it. Family is meant to be *for* you, not against you. Family *can* be so much more, but the key to overcoming this is to move on from toxic individuals as soon as possible, even if they are your blood relatives. Create the space you need in your life to thrive and maintain a healthy balance in all your relationships.

7) HOPELESSNESS

When I was a child, the adults taught me to pay attention in class, respect your elders, and work hard at doing your best. I was a well-behaved kid from kindergarten through ninth grade. I remember trying out for sports and signing up for my first spelling bee. If the activity was open and looked fun, I wanted to take part. I didn't mind staying after school to participate in activities. I looked forward to the challenge. It was this or go home to face the monsters there. I preferred the new and challenging over the old and all-too-familiar pain.

I never understood why I had such a powerful drive to overachieve at such a young age. As I matured, I realized it was a way to block out the pain of the things I dealt with at home. Working hard at school and joining extracurricular activities became a way of life for me from age seven to twelve. It was my way of overcoming all the inappropriate touching and name calling that happened all too often at that age. I learned how to compartmentalize and cope with the pain with a combination of willpower, hard work, and smart avoidance.

> *The best way not to feel hopeless is to get up and do something.*
>
> **— Barack Obama**

Keeping myself busy was an art that helped me block out the pain and keep me distracted from the negative interactions at home. Overachieving and striving to be the best at my craft was my focus, and it pulled me through. I didn't get many accolades or pats on the back from family or friends, but I didn't need this as motivation. Sure, it would have been nice, but I learned not to expect love and support. I manifested hope for myself by working hard and never giving up.

Not everything painful or difficult will stay that way forever. This too shall pass. Hopefulness follows hopelessness. It's a cycle and you need only wait for things to turn around. Have hope that life doesn't have to be as it is right now. There is a light at the end of the tunnel. Keep heading in the direction your heart is leading you.

I firmly believe all seven of these roadblocks will challenge everyone. Likely, you've either faced these, are facing these, or will face them at some point. There's no avoiding a challenging life. There's no such thing as an easy pass. You WILL face trials and tribulations of all kinds. The book of James chapter 1 says:

Consider it pure joy, my brothers and sisters, whenever you face trials of many kinds, because you know that the testing of your faith produces perseverance. Let perseverance finish its work so that you may be mature and complete, not lacking anything. [Jas 1:2-4 NIV]

These challenges will come in full force when you least expect it. If your goal is to make treasure from trash and overcome life's many obstacles, get wise to what's coming your way. Prepare and get ready to fight for love. Keep the faith and keep tackling your obstacles day by day.

PRACTICING ENDLESS LOVE

- **Pray:** *Lord, move in me. Help me see my struggles for what they are; nothing you cannot overcome. Help me overcome and to rise above. Don't leave me in the valley. I plead with you to lead me out and bring me to greener pastures. Show me love by leading me as you would a child. Wipe away my pain, my tears, and all my doubts. Give me the strength to say no to those who I can no longer help. Give me wisdom to soar above the valley and to discover a path out. Lead me to you, Lord, in all things. Teach me to listen and to seek you. Amen!*

- **Read:** If you're looking for some perspective on your life circumstance and situation, the book, *Insanity of God,* by Nik Ripken certainly delivers. It tells the story of a husband-and-wife missionary team who get a firsthand look at the horrors of third world countries like Somalia. It is a story of hope that even despite incredible difficulties and trials, God will never leave us.

- **Act:** Stay vigilant against Cyber Illusion, one of the most invasive roadblocks. Put the phone down. Limit your time spent looking at a screen, especially before bed. Set a timer on your phone to alert you when it's 10 p.m. and time to shut it down. Do this once a week at first and work up to doing it regularly as a habit. Adjust your phone's settings to limit your exposure to blue light. Keep your phone in the other room when you don't really need it. Buy a basic alarm clock so you don't have to sleep near your phone. Turn your notifications off and put your phone on silent mode unless you're expecting an important call. We've fooled ourselves into thinking that we need our phone by our side 24/7. It's just not true. Destroy the lie.

CONCLUSION
THRIVING IN LOVE

Finally, brothers, rejoice. Aim for restoration, comfort one another, agree with one another, live in peace; and the God of love and peace will be with you. [2 Corinthians 13:11 ESV]

This has been my story of Endless Love. Love does not stop when we're no longer in each other's lives. If you had to walk away from relatives or close friends love is still there (it never dies). I have learned through adversities you discover your strength. Your relationships will be tested. If you're able to stand through the pain and the challenges, you will come out stronger.

In my marital relationship we struggled with selfless love because we both came from dysfunctional households. We fought our way through to overcome seemingly insurmountable odds. The periods of long-suffering for both of us forced us to be more selfless, forgiving, and focused as a team. I had to learn to forgive, trust, have patience, and show grace. He had to learn how to forgive, lead with kindness, and actively listen. We are stronger now than ever because we were forged by fire, and we are still growing each day.

Several years ago, while our children were still young, my husband and I separated. It was a difficult time in our relationship, and I didn't see myself moving forward in the marriage. Not only did we struggle in our marriage, but we also had a challenging time agreeing on how to raise our children. I saw life one way, and he saw life another way. We both had valid points with how to raise kids and maintain a balanced household. But we both lacked maturity, experience, or understanding. We didn't know how to compromise or meet each other halfway. Everything was a fight and an argument, and some arguments lasted for days.

Each day is a process, and mending broken hearts takes time, willingness, patience, and forgiveness. Our children suffered because of our poor behavior towards one another. It affected them emotionally, mentally, and caused them to be defiant and lash out. It has been a lot of work getting our family on track and it requires selflessness and sacrifice.

> I was determined my children were worth the fight, the sacrifice, and the hurt. When I wanted to choose me, I chose them. This is "Endless Love."

When I wanted to give up and walk away, I pressed in harder. I prayed more; I fasted more, and I believed more. It was my primary goal to provide stability for my children. It has been challenging, but I'm grateful for the good and the bad experiences. Those experiences have made me who I am today. I am still learning and growing; each day I look at myself and ask, "how can I be a better person?"

I am thankful to this day that I listened, and I trusted God's plan for my life. We don't always get a second chance in life, and God's way is not always easy. There will be times God will direct you to do things you don't want to do. But if you follow the voice of God, you will have a better result. I am learning today to have blind faith, even when I don't understand. I am learning to trust the process and know that my creator loves me, cares for me, and desires the very best for me.

I still don't understand how a lot of things worked out, but the more time I spend with God, the more He reveals the mystery of heaven to me. He showed me the power of Endless Love and I followed the path He laid out before me.

In the darkest times of my life is where I learned what Endless Love really means. I learned that our timing matters much less than God's. Our trials are not meant to break us they are designed to make us.

Not all relationships can or should have a positive ending. If you're in a relationship that takes away from you and does not add to you; it's time to go. We all have purpose and those you are connected to either push you into your purpose or pull you away from your purpose. I'm not suggesting you should get back together or reconnect with someone in your life if they've hurt you deeply. Time and self-work absolutely can heal all wounds, but as I've mentioned before, letting go and moving on is an okay step to take. But always be open to God's timing if He wants to bring you back. What I'm suggesting and hoping for you is that you listen for the voice of God, whether he is telling you to reconnect or stay away. Try to avoid being extreme and so set in your ways that you can't hear from God.

> I'm passionate about the ultimate redemptive power of Endless Love. If you stay the course and don't give up, anything is possible for you!

You have the power to rekindle important family ties, reconnect with friends that have hurt you, and restore broken relationships to their previous levels of love and intimacy. If you lead with love, there is nothing that can stand in your way.

7 FINAL TAKEAWAYS TO ENDLESS LOVE

In keeping with the theme of this book, I want to offer seven quick takeaways for living in Endless Love. If you get nothing else out of this book, I want you to come away with at least one actionable strategy that will change your life if you follow through and do the hard work. Read and take action to become a more loving person.

1. **Always put God first:** God should be the ultimate authority in your life and the one you spend the most time with. His voice is the voice you want to listen to above all others. As you grow in relationship with your Creator, you will filter out the other loud and competing voices in your everyday life. God will become the one voice that rises above all others, and you will learn to trust in Him with all of your heart, mind, and soul.

2. **Develop spiritual disciplines to grow in relationship with God:** Work on your spiritual disciplines to hear from God and to learn how to best live out your faith. Grow in self-awareness and focus on what you need to do to overcome any struggles or to improve upon your new lessons. Read the Bible, pray, and go to your knees as you cry out for God. Ask Him to show you what Endless Love means and ask Him for access. Show up and take it one day at a time but always move forward.

3. **Love yourself unconditionally:** Love yourself no matter what. You are unique, wonderful, and special. Each person is perfect in God's eyes. As you begin to understand God's amazing love for all, learn to love yourself the same way. Don't neglect your own needs if you're feeling a major drop in energy or motivation. Treat yourself well. Make time for you so you can be there for others.

4. **Practice self-love strategies:** Self-love is not selfish. Showing yourself love by doing self-care activities is vital for your endurance. The only way to love over the long haul is to keep up your own strength. Keep your own cup full before helping others. Don't compare yourself to other people who might be ahead of you. Develop into the person God wants you to become but start slow and don't rush the process.

5. **Have a zestful love for others:** Show love to your friends, family, and to your community. Celebrate the uniqueness of each individual by learning which love languages they speak. Treat each person differently, according to what you know to be true about them. Take action out in the real world and don't ignore the moments God speaks to your heart to be there for others. Whether it's a close family member or someone in need on the street, learn to show others Endless Love through your actions. And when all else fails and things get really difficult, just be there. Show up and be a shoulder to cry on. Sometimes loving others is as simple as that.

6. **Understand we are all different:** All of our interactions will benefit if we take this simple yet complicated truth to heart. The people around you might not look like you, talk like you, or think like you. Recognize the unique individuality of each person and get to know

people as they are. Treat each person and their differences with love and respect.

7. **Don't succumb to common roadblocks:** Make treasure out of whatever trash might come your way. Use
your newfound ability to love more deeply to leap over
roadblocks or smash through them. Make progress in
your life by never settling for less than your absolute
best. Make your life extraordinary and don't be afraid to
reach for more than you currently have.

WRAPPING UP AND MOVING FORWARD: LIVING IN LOVE

I hope my words made an impact. Now it's your turn. I challenge you to love more deeply today. Take action on one or two
takeaways you've learned. Don't let this book sit on your
nightstand or bookshelf without having gotten something out
of it. Take action born of the desire to love others, to repair broken relationships, make new friends, give back to your community, change hearts, or make someone's day just when they
needed it the most.

Even if you've gotten to this point and only have a bit more
hope in your heart for the endless splendor of love, I count this
book as a success.

I want you to know you are loved, valuable, and incredible.

Your story isn't written in stone. Each day is yet another day to take a step forward in love.

I'm happy you made the commitment to learn more about Love. Remember that God is the ultimate authority, and I hope you read more from His word. I am merely a conduit for His vast and Endless Love. The verses throughout this book were some of the best I've found to showcase God's incredible love for you and all His creation. But don't stop there! Get into his word, grow in your spiritual disciplines, and keep on shining bright.

Lastly, trials are not meant to break you, they are designed to make you. Destiny is born out of trials and pain. Most of us discover our purpose during a trial. Let this book and many others be a source of comfort as you become a better version of you.

Endless Love is available to you and the people in your life. You simply need to reach out and grab it.

Best of wishes and much love,

—**Angela**

AFFIRMATIONS

Use these uplifting daily affirmations to improve positive thinking and to place yourself in a posture of prayer before God. Learning to love takes daily practice and a small commitment of time. Some days will be easier than others, but don't miss out on the opportunity to affirm a great day ahead.

FORGIVENESS

Letting go of past hurts and removing all bitterness from your heart.

- Today is a brand-new day. This is a new beginning. I am strong and ready to show love no matter what happened in the past. I will love today even in a small way.

- I will let the past be in the past. I release the hurt and pain from yesterday. Today is a new and wonderful day.

- I forgive those who have hurt me and caused me pain. I will approach them with fresh eyes and a heart for love.

- I pray that I am forgiven for hurting others and causing them pain. I ask God to give me a heart free of pain and burden of the past.

- I choose to forgive and let them go. I am strong and do not need them in order to thrive.

- I choose to love. I choose to seek wisdom and understanding from God.

- I choose to make better choices, and that starts today. I will put God first and ask for his blessing on each of my actions.

- I choose to love others where they are and not where I think they should be.

- I choose to forgive myself for bad choices and for allowing people to treat me poorly and for rewarding their destructive behavior.

- I choose to love, cherish, and honor me today. If I am not well, then I am unable to help others. I must start with myself.

- I forgive and I let go!!!

OPPORTUNITY

We have more potential than we know. Each day is a new opportunity to show love.

- This is the day that the Lord has made. I will rejoice and be glad in it.

- Today, good things will happen for me and to me. I choose to be authentic.

- Today, I will be an example of God's presence on the earth. I have heaven's favor in my life.

- I am blessed. It is God's will that I do well, be well and prosper in the earth.

- I am destined for greatness. All the experiences, education, and skills I have will be used to prosper me on the earth.

- My God desires that I do well and prosper. No weapon formed against me shall prosper.

- I am the elect of God. I will and shall recover all that has been taken from me.

- I am positioned for success and ready for new opportunities.

NEW BEGINNINGS

Healing and wholeness are available to me, and I will begin anew today.

- I choose to freely love and to freely give. I have new energy given by God to give of myself today.

- I choose to be optimistic, affectionate, carefree, and authentic today.

- I will no longer dwell on past hurt and pain.

- I no longer seek revenge or attention from individuals that choose to hate. I will let them go if that's what I need to do.

- Today I choose me. I am open to love. I am open to giving. I am open to forgiving and letting go.

- I am open to new opportunities for success. I will stay cognizant of how I might influence these opportunities, and I will not miss things that come my way.

- I am healed, and I am whole. My mind is healthy, strong, and sound. My heart is healthy and strong.

- My blood is flowing through my heart properly. My emotions are healthy and balanced. My body is healthy and strong. The foods I eat today will strengthen my body and give me energy to do what I need to do today.

- I am financially healthy and strong. I have more than enough. I will continue to give away more than I should, because God will take care of me.

- I am spiritually and emotionally mature and stable. I will put God first today in everything that I do.

- I am whole and I am the strongest I have ever been. I feel capable of tackling whatever the world throws at me today. I will overcome even the most difficult roadblocks.

COUNTLESS LOVE

I will count my endless blessings. Each person I meet deserves countless love.

- I will ask the people around me; how can I love you more?

- I choose to see clearly with eyes of love, and I love what I see.

- I will draw love and romance into my life, and I accept it now.

- I will notice love around every corner and let joy fill my entire world.

- I deserve love from myself and my inner circle and will find new love and new experiences in life and joy in every breath and moment.

- I rejoice in the love I receive every day.

- I will remove evil doing and talking from the internal and external environment.

- I will pour love into all encounters with every spirit I meet.

- I will be caring and compassionate in my personal relationships.

- I will be slow to anger and quicker to love.

- My spiritual and lifetime partner will find me and will love me unconditionally and grow with me on a spiritual, emotional, physical, and financial level.

- My spiritual partner will love God, and will love to be married, and will be a loving, caring, and giving person.

- I will continue to be strong and walk in God's path and shine light into the darkest areas of people's heart and soul.

- I will continue to love myself unconditionally with no judgment and no hatred.

CONTROL

My thoughts are my own, and I will be in control of my mind.

- I will not pass judgment on people or myself, and I will operate with good intention.

- From this day on, I will allow no one to have control over my emotions or thoughts.

- I will not allow outside, or bad influences control my thoughts, my thoughts of self-care, self-love, and reverence.

- I will not let any being control my path with God by their comments, actions, or persuasion.

- I will control my thoughts and focus on purpose, positivity, and love, and practice self-control of anger, rage, and impatience.

- No other spirit will control my spirit.

I APOLOGIZE

I will apologize to myself for any wrongdoings and will own my part in any troubles.

- I am sorry for the hurt and pain I have caused you.

- I am sorry for letting you down. I am sorry for not protecting you.

- I am sorry for making poor decisions. I am sorry for all the time I doubted you.

- I am sorry for not honoring you, loving you, or caring for you.

- You are so BEAUTIFUL. Your heart is so gentle and so big.

- You have such a beautiful mind. You possess a tenacity for life.

- God created you for a noble purpose. You are destined for great things.

- It is a privilege and honor to be me.

- You are a beautiful person. Thank you for not giving up on me.

- Thank you for being strong.

- I love you.

- Never give up on yourself.

- Never apologize for being your authentic, wonderful self!

MORE THAN ENOUGH

You are more than enough, just as you are.

- I love you so much. I wanted to let you know you are worth the fight.

- You are precious.

- There is no amount of money that can buy you.

- I love your beautiful mind, your courage and how you dream.

- I love how you chase life and your strength.

- You are a powerful person. Never let your circumstances stop you from moving forward.

- God has blessed you with so many gifts.

- No matter how you feel right now, no matter how it looks, your future is better than your past.

- Your future is bright. God has big things in store for you.

- Let go of things and people that gave up on you.

- God loves you and desires the best for you.

- You are worth the fight. You are more than enough.

- I am sorry you are hurting. I am sorry for the lack of support you have not received.

- But you are loved, you are wanted, and you are desired.

- You are more than enough.

- I love you so much.

- God has so many things in store for you.

- Prepare to receive the blessings that will be poured into your life.

- Stay beautiful, hopeful, and ready to receive. You have everything you need to be successful. You are More Than Enough!!!

PRAYERS

Prayer is a conversation with God. Practice opening your heart and telling Him what you need and want from life. You do not have to understand how it works, (the power of prayer is incredible but hard to grasp!) so just start talking to Him. You will grow in connection and prayer ability over time, but for now, keep it really simple and just start talking.

May this section be a guide for you as you begin your prayer journey. You do not have to say these prayers verbatim, but may they be a starting place for you as you start to feel, practice, and emulate Endless Love.

FORGIVENESS

Thank you for saving me and forgiving me of all my sins. Help me let go of any hurt from my past. Help me overcome the darkness in my heart and the feelings of pain, hatred, resentment, and impurity that rises in my soul when I think about them and what they did. Help me to overcome this pain and to let it all go. Help me to forgive them just as you forgave me, my God. Lead me to you and fill me up with your endless love. Cleanse me from within and remove any negative thoughts. Help me to think more about you. Amen.

OPPORTUNITY

Thank you for opening extraordinary doors that no one can close. Thank you for closing the wrong doors that are not opened by you. Help me to keep walking in the direction you want me to go, even if I have no idea why. Give me the ability to trust you, no matter what. Show me the opportunities you want me to seek and light my path all the way there. Help me when I stay and guide me back to you like a lost sheep. Never forget me, Lord! Show me how I can be more loving and how I can become the best version of myself. Thank you! Amen.

THANKFULNESS

Thank you for caring for me. Thank you for loving me. Thank you to all the beautiful people in my life. Thank you for not leaving me. Thank you for saving me. Thank you for a sound mind. Thank you, that my thoughts are clear, and I make wise decisions. Thank you for your love, honor, and favor. Today I will be joyful, hopeful and at peace. Thank you for all you have done for me. Amen.

COUNTLESS LOVE

Lord, help me be patient as I wait for love. Help me to see and appreciate the love all around me. Help me wait for the right people to enter my life that you want me to show love to. Lift up my spirit and guide me to take action in the real world. Help me to be more loving to all of those I meet. Show me who needs me and push me toward them. Don't let me get away with excuses for inaction. Keep my spirit filled with passionate love for others. Help me to want the best for them and to be able to lead them to you with my actions. Amen.

CONTROL

I surrender control to you, my God. I cannot do this alone. Life is really hard right now and I don't know what to do. Everything seems like a mess. I'm in great need of you. I need you in every way and in each area of my life. I give up control of my work, my family, and all of my goals. I look to you and I trust in you, my God. Love me. Show me love. Help me out of the troubles I am in and show me a future without as much pain and difficulty. Help me to trust you. Amen.

MORE THAN ENOUGH

God, help me to know that I am more than enough. Build me up and teach me how to enter self-discovery. Show me how to love myself and how to believe in myself. Grant me an inner power to glow. Let me be someone who knows my value and knows how to share your love with others in my unique way. Help me to embrace my weaknesses. Enhance my strengths. Open up my heart and mind to the person you want me to become. Amen!

LIVING IN LOVE

Lord, help me to put together everything I've learned in this book about living in love. Lead me to read from your word to embrace these truths for myself. Put me in situations that demand that I live in love. Always be with me as I learn the power of Endless Love and I find healing in my relationships. Lord, you are good and mighty. Help me to be humble and to always come to you on my knees seeking your wisdom and grace. Thank you, Lord, for all you've done for me. Amen.

A QUICK FAVOR?

Before you go, can I ask you for a quick favor? Would you please leave this book a review?

Reviews are very important for authors, and your honest feedback can help others find me. Please leave the book a review today wherever you may have purchased it.

Thank you for reading and thank you for joining me on this adventure.

-Angela

THANK YOU AND GOD BLESS!

Thank you for reading Endless Love. I hope this book has been a blessing upon your heart. I hope it has sprinkled tidbits of hope and wisdom into your life and onto your heart.

Let's keep the conversation going. Please visit my website and connect with me at:

WWW.COUNTLESSLOVE.COM

OR

ANGELA-MOORE@COUNTLESSLOVE.COM

I can't wait to hear from you!

- Angela

ABOUT THE AUTHOR

Angela was born and raised in Washington D.C. She is a passionate Author, Speaker, Technologist, and Health coach. She has a

natural passion for the arts, fitness, music, and outreach. Angela finds joy in the performing arts, and community outreach. She has implemented an after-school youth groups in her local community where she also acted as a youth counselor for years. She has participated in several local outreach programs and ministries.

She later discovered her passion for technology. Angela received her Bachelor of Science in Computer Information Systems from University of Maryland University College. She started her technology career as an Engineer where she later became a Senior level consultant in the industry. As Angela's love for technology grew, she mentored and taught others in her field.

She has counseled and mentored through local youth programs, women's entrepreneur programs and through individual counseling.

She is an advocate for organic food and holistic healing. Her love for agriculture and nature stems from North Carolina where her grandfather owned and operated a farm. She used food and fitness to heal and overcome significant trials in her life. She believes that fitness is mental, emotional, psychological, and physical. She now owns and operate a health and wellness business where she teaches and coaches others how to use holistic methods to heal the body, mind, and overcome adverse circumstances.